LIVING A

A PRACTICAL GUIDE TO UNDERSTANDING SEXUAL SIN AND BIBLICAL ANSWERS FOR BREAKING SIN'S POWER.

JOHN COBLENTZ

Christian Light Publications, Inc.

Harrisonburg, Virginia 22802

LIVING A PURE LIFE

Christian Light Publications, Inc.
Harrisonburg, Virginia 22802
© 2007 by Christian Light Publications, Inc.
All rights reserved. Published 2007
Printed in the United States of America

CLP's policy is to use the King James Version of the Bible except in cases, such as this book, when a few verses from another translation may be quoted for clarity.

Cover design:
Joseph Ebersole / Illustra Graphics
Myerstown, Pennsylvania

ISBN: 978-0-87813-649-0

CONTENTS

Foreword v

1. Understanding Temptation 1

2. Understanding Sexual Temptation 19

3. Identifying Underlying Issues 39

4. Repenting of Moral Failure 55

5. Rebuilding Moral Character 71

6. Working Through Consequences 99

7. Living a Pure Life 123

Appendix A: The Problem of Masturbation 145

Appendix B: Homosexuality 167

Appendix C: Restoring Purity in Women 185

Endnotes 199

FOREWORD

In my twelve years as a marriage counselor, I repeatedly faced such sins as adultery, fornication, incest, masturbation, pornography, and sexual exploitation of children. Less frequently, but still too often, I helped people struggling with sexual deviations such as homosexuality, bestiality, and sexual fixations. The personal and relational effects of these sins can hardly be put into words. Sin carries incredible price tags.

In spite of the sorrows that attend sexual sins, they continue to hold many attractions for both men and women. A man can know he is wrecking his family, destroying his character, and bringing shame to the name of Christ and still go back again and again into the very sins that are doing the damage.

Thank God there is grace!

This book is a compilation of the principles and guidance we have from the Word of God regarding moral purity. It faces honestly what happens when we sin. It lays out the requirements for dealing with sexual sin. And it points the way to living a pure life. Several appendices deal with particular issues that are not common to all.

This is not a storybook. Stories of sexual sin, even when the consequences are named, tend to catch the ears of our fleshly interests and sometimes do more damage than good. In the few cases I did discuss, I changed the names and recounted only the details necessary to make my point. On the other hand, I am grateful to God for including the stories in His Word that show us not only how people fell into sin, but how He brought them out. They give us hope. For no matter how far we have fallen, where there is true penitence, there is adequate grace. God still saves from sin. God still changes lives.

In the moral chaos of our times, we need the clear call to moral purity. Amidst all the evidence that sexual sin destroys relationships, we need testimonies that moral purity preserves relationships and testimonies that divine grace changes lives. It is my prayer that this book will lead many in the paths of righteousness, that it will call many from the ruins of unrighteousness, and that it will honor God—to whom alone belong the kingdom and the power and the glory forever!

—John Coblentz

1

UNDERSTANDING
TEMPTATION

"Let no man say when he is tempted,
I am tempted of God:
for God cannot be tempted with evil,
neither tempteth he any man:
But every man is tempted,
when he is drawn away
of his own lust, and enticed.
Then when lust hath conceived,
it bringeth forth sin:
and sin, when it is finished,
bringeth forth death."
James 1:13-15

The above verses show us that temptation is an attractive invitation to a fatal process. It can be reduced to an equation: Desire + attractive (but poisonous) offer = suffering → death. In other words, a person has a desire and sees something that looks like it could satisfy that desire. He takes what he sees and finds temporary relief, but suddenly he begins to experience serious consequences that, unless there is intervention, result in death.

This process can be illustrated in countless ways. A hungry man is offered a plate of delicious food. He doesn't know that it is contaminated with poison. He eats with delight. But a few hours later he begins to feel intestinal discomfort. With no medical help, he is soon writhing in pain. And shortly, he is dead.

Leon was a young man with normal desires for acceptance and friendship. He turned to friends, however, whose activities were laced with sin. Leon eventually began doing drugs and chasing women. His racy lifestyle brought complications, including fights with rival drug addicts and, of course, it also brought the disapproval of his parents. One morning, to the horror of his friends and family, Leon was found shot in his apartment. It was never fully resolved if his death was a homicide or a suicide. Leon had been led away into sin by his desires, and the end product of sin was his ruin. Truly, temptation is an attractive invitation to a fatal process.

In spite of James's clear teaching about temptation, there are many misunderstandings about it. Have you ever heard any of these comments?

- *I just couldn't help myself.*
- *I never would have done it if she hadn't _____.*
- *Why did God even allow me to be in a place of temptation?*
- *I don't know what got into me!*

In all these examples, we see how squeamish we are about taking personal responsibility for our sin. We tend to think of temptation as something that comes to us totally from outside of us. We seem to feel better if we can pass the responsibility on to others, to our circumstances, to the devil, and even to God. But James shows us that temptation starts in our own hearts. If we are going to overcome temptation, we need to start looking at it God's way.

TEMPTATION IS INSEPARABLY LINKED TO DESIRE.

"Every man is tempted, when he is drawn away of his own lust" (James 1:14). The word *lust* in English has negative connotations. But the Greek word is used for both good and bad desires. The real problem is not that we have desires, or even that we have wrong desires, but that our desires are focused on the wrong things or on the wrong ways of satisfying the desires.

To be alive is to have desires. A dead person has no desire and therefore cannot be tempted. But because we are alive, our enemy can play on our desires to lead us astray. He urged Eve to fulfill the longing to be wiser. He stirred up David's desire for intimacy and pleasure. He played on the rich young ruler's desire for recognition and significance, or perhaps for security, in riches.

No matter what the objective may be or what is held before our eyes, the temptation rides on an inflamed desire.

GOD HAS GUIDELINES FOR HOW WE SATISFY OUR DESIRES.

As our Creator, God not only designed us with appetites and desires, but He also has given us guidelines for how we satisfy those desires. There is a right reason for eating, a proper relationship for sex, and right ways of building friendship; and because there are right ways of satisfying our desires, there are also countless wrong ways to pursue them.

The Bible warns against violating God's guidelines even

for such common appetites as food and drink. Solomon wrote, "Blessed art thou, O land, when thy king is the son of nobles, and thy princes eat in due season, for strength, and not for drunkenness!" (Ecclesiastes 10:17).

Many more guidelines are given to keep the desire for sexual pleasure in its place—warnings against fornication, adultery, homosexuality, bestiality, sexual abuse, even warnings against joking about such matters. "But fornication, and all uncleanness, or covetousness, let it not be once named among you, as becometh saints; neither filthiness, nor foolish talking, nor jesting, which are not convenient: but rather giving of thanks. For this ye know, that no whoremonger, nor unclean person, nor covetous man, who is an idolater, hath any inheritance in the kingdom of Christ and of God" (Ephesians 5:3-5).

God's guidelines are not to torment us or to withhold good things from us (as Satan suggests). Rather, He places restrictions and guidelines on our desires in order to preserve for us the most healthy and blessed way of satisfying them. He knows that if we choose adultery, for example, we will ruin our marriages. If we seek security in things, we will not experience the joy of trust in the Father. If we are gluttonous or drunken, we will not only increase health problems for ourselves, but will also make our lives less enjoyable and our bodies less able to carry out our responsibilities. If we learn to control sexual urges in our youth, we strengthen our ability to remain faithful in marriage. So God gives these guidelines to protect us.

WE HAVE DESIRES AT DIFFERENT LEVELS OF OUR BEING.

When we think about the wide range of human desires,

we can readily see that our desires operate on different levels. We have hunger and thirst on a physical level. We have a sexual drive, which, although it is physical in its manifestation, is deeply rooted in who we are as persons. On an emotional level, we hunger for acceptance, for belonging, for roots, for security, and for friendship. These hungers, although less tangible than the hunger for food or drink, are sometimes even more powerful. On a deeper level still, we long for something or someone to believe in, for something to give our lives to, for an object of devotion and worship.

All these desires in the root sense are not wrong.

Temptation is enticement to satisfy these desires in wrong ways, at the wrong time, or for the wrong reasons.

For example, Jesus was tempted to turn stones into food. The hunger for food was not wrong, but He was tempted to satisfy His appetite for the wrong reason—to prove that He was the Son of God (see Matthew 4:3).

Notice also that in temptation, our desires often overlap. We may eat (physical desire) to satisfy a hunger for recognition (emotional desire)—as the teenage boy who eats ten hamburgers at a sitting with his friends gawking in amazement. We may want sex or we may give in to sexual pressure to gain acceptance. We may seek God in order to be looked up to. Any desire—however legitimate or good in itself—can be an avenue into sin. We are constantly tempted to satisfy our desires in some illegitimate way or for some selfish reason.

THERE IS AN ORDER OF PRIORITY IN OUR DESIRES.

Although we have many desires, not all desires are equal. Or stated another way, our desires have an order of priority. The hunger for food is not as important as the hunger for friendship; and the hunger for friendship is not as important as the hunger for an object of worship or devotion.

Many temptations come to us as enticement to satisfy desires for things of lesser importance at the expense of desires for things of greater importance—for example, we may be tempted to feed physical appetites at the expense of the soul. Thus, when Esau sold his birthright for a bowl of soup, he had his priorities all turned around. He satisfied a superficial hunger at the expense of his family honor. And when Judas sold his Lord for silver, he made a horrendous trade-off. He surrendered his soul for clinking coins. By putting money at the place of his heart's devotion, he was feeding the deepest longing of the heart with rubbish.

But lest we be too hard on Esau and Judas, we need to realize that we face the same temptations they did. We are constantly urged to sacrifice our friendships, our family relationships—our very souls—for trinkets or for a moment's pleasure. Our desires for things tangible continually stand ready to lead us astray on matters of the heart.

FOR FURTHER STUDY:

1. What is the "formula" for temptation?

2. The death resulting from sin is not simply physical (as in the example of Leon). Sin may cause the death of a relationship or the death of a life goal. Can you list other "deaths" that result when we yield to sin?

3. Can you give examples from your own life, or from people you have known, where sin led to death?

4. Think about the sexual temptations you have faced. List one (or several) of your strongest temptations.

5. Supposing you would yield to this temptation, what

would you sacrifice in the process? Be as specific as you can.

6. What guidelines of God speak to your temptation(s)? Write out several verses.

UNDER CERTAIN CIRCUMSTANCES, WE ARE MORE VULNERABLE TO TEMPTATION.

Desires do not remain constant. We are more tempted to ignore God's directions for our appetites when we are hungry than when we are full. This is such an obvious point we often miss it. But the reality is that deprivation increases vulnerability. A starving person will not pay much attention to whether food is healthful or properly prepared or even fit to eat.

This principle is not as consequential with food as it is when applied to deeper levels of hunger. The person who has been rejected all his life, when presented with attention and acceptance, may show no more discretion than a famished man who is presented with food. And so, the teenager starving for friends will be beset by strong temptations—he is so hungry, he cares little how the hunger is satisfied. The deep hunger makes him more vulnerable to violating God's standards for friendship.

But hunger is not the only thing that increases desire. Yielding to temptation ironically has the same effect. Every normal human being faces sexual temptation in growing up— that is, he/she faces the urge to satisfy sexual desire in wrong ways. But *if* he yields to temptation and *the more* he yields to temptation, the stronger the temptation becomes.

And this is true precisely because temptation is enticement to satisfy desires in wrong ways. That is, satisfying our desires as God intended provides a sense of satisfaction (both in the fulfillment of desire and in the approval of our conscience) that never can be found in following temptation. When we gratify a desire wrongly, we are always left with an emptiness, an ache that tells us something is wrong. Of course, gratifying a desire wrongly may give a temporary satisfaction, even a thrill, but instead of satisfying the heart, it leaves the heart more empty. That growing emptiness over time results in stronger temptation. A man who tries to fill his desire for recognition through financial gain likely will make money—and making money may bring him a temporary sense of happiness—an illusion of fulfillment. But that happiness won't be the kind of heart-satisfaction that he would have, for example, in being recognized for his character. By indulging in moneymaking, he increases the emptiness of his heart; and as the lust for money grows, he may resort to cheating, dishonest deals, and sacrificing his relationships as well as his character. The emptiness grows and the temptations strengthen because God never intended for the human heart to be satisfied with money. Likely there was a time when Judas would have forthrightly rejected the temptation to betray his Lord for money. But as he yielded to temptation little by little, eventually he could not say no to opportunity, even at the terrible price he paid.

Thus, wherever we transgress the ways of God, we lay a trap for ourselves in future temptations. Sin can be forgiven in a moment, but by that sin we have weakened our ability to resist sinning in the same way (or in a similar way) at a later point. This is the nature of sin and temptation. A man or woman can be saved at any point no matter how far down the path of sin they have gone, but the further down the path they go, the fewer there are who turn around. As the temptations become stronger, the ease of sinning increases proportionally. This does not mean the power of sin cannot be broken. Praise God for grace! But it does call us to be sober about sin and its consequences.

TEMPTATION OPERATES ON PREMISES OF DECEPTION.

Whenever it looks attractive to ignore or violate God's guidelines for satisfying our desires, something is skewed. Good is made to look bad, and bad is made to look good. What is fleeting is made to appear more important than what is enduring, and the other way around. We think we will *get* when in reality we will *lose*. This is the nature of temptation and sin.

Satan, of course, is the mastermind of temptation. He knows how to offer the world on platters of silver . . . and rob us blind in the process.

People in the Far North devised a way to kill wolves in a singularly chilling way. They embedded razor blades in chunks of meat and attached the meat to stakes in the ice. The hungry wolves would lick and gnaw the meat and eventually expose the razor blades, cutting their tongues and lips. The fresh blood increased their craze for meat, resulting in more cuts and more blood. Driven by the taste of their own blood, they would keep eating and bleeding until they died.

These are Satan's tactics too. If he can whet our desire, he can get us to want—to feverishly chase after—what actually destroys us.

A friend of mine who commonly travels in Third-World countries told me he has made it a policy not to exchange money on the street. The risk of getting short-changed is simply too high. But one day he was caught needing money after the banks were closed, so he decided to go against his better judgment "this one time."

He asked a moneylender nearby if he could change a one-hundred-dollar bill. The moneylender was affability itself. "Certainly! No problem!" My friend watched carefully as he counted out the money.

The moneylender then said, "Oh, actually, would you have two fifties instead of the one-hundred-dollar bill? The hundred-dollar bill is harder for me to use."

My friend checked his billfold, and sure enough, he had two fifties. It made no difference to him, so they traded bills, and my friend quickly put his hundred in his pocket for safekeeping.

The moneylender gave the money to my friend and said, "Count it and make sure it is right." My friend did so. It was correct.

The moneylender took the money and counted it one more time to be absolutely sure. Then he gave my friend the money.

As the moneylender turned away, a couple of things happened. Several other people jostled into my friend as he took the money, distracting him. But he again unfolded the wad of bills to check them before he put them away. To his dismay, he saw that only the outside bill was money. The remainder was folded paper. He looked up to find the moneylender, but, of course, he was gone. And the people milling around made it impossible to move quickly to find the man.

Realizing he had been cheated, my friend reached into his pocket to check the one-hundred-dollar bill he had repocketed in the exchange. He pulled it out, and was stunned to find that it was a one-dollar bill.

He had lost nearly two hundred dollars in less than five minutes, even while paying careful attention not to be cheated.

This is the way of Satan. When we decide to deal with him,

he short-changes us. Every time! He is skilled at making us feel like doing something "this one time," getting us to drop our guard, making us believe we will gain, and then taking everything we have.

Temptation always operates on premises of deception.

FOR FURTHER STUDY:

1. Name the two conditions that increase desire.
2. In your own experience, which of these would you consider more significant in increasing the pull of temptation?
3. Read Isaiah 5:20. List some of the methods Satan uses in our culture to twist the truth about sexual sin.
4. Of the methods you listed, which has had the most influence on your own life?

SATAN USES A VARIETY OF MEANS TO TRY TO GET BELIEVERS TO FALL.

We have already noted that Satan is a master at deception. As Jesus said, "When he lies, he speaks his native language, for he is a liar and the father of lies" (John 8:44, NIV).[1] Deception, however, is not Satan's only tactic. He comes often as an "angel of light" (2 Corinthians 11:14), but when that tactic does not work, he may come as a "roaring lion" (1 Peter 5:8). That is, he may mount special attacks against those who are faithful to resist temptation.

The Apostle Paul spoke of a "thorn in the flesh" that he begged God to remove. He termed it "the messenger of Satan to buffet me" (2 Corinthians 12:7). Apparently, this involved physical distress (it was in his "flesh") and was specifically a means of Satan to harass him and make his life miserable.

Satan is a thief—he comes "to steal, and to kill, and to destroy" (John 10:10). His intent is to break down believers in any way he can, to take from us anything valuable, to wear down our resistance, and to make us think a situation is hopeless.

In times of harassment and distress, we may be tempted to become discouraged. We may begin to doubt that God loves us, to question His wisdom in allowing distress in our lives, and even to give up. Some believers who have resisted Satan's temptations to satisfy the desires of the flesh have fallen into discouragement when facing trials and hardships.

Thus, in the New Testament, "temptation" and "trial" are closely related. "My brethren, count it all joy when ye fall into divers temptations; knowing this, that the trying of your faith worketh patience" (James 1:2, 3). Or as Peter wrote, "Wherein ye greatly rejoice, though now for a season, if need be, ye are in heaviness through manifold temptations: that the trial of your faith, being much more precious than of gold that perisheth, though it be tried with fire, might be found unto praise and honour and glory at the appearing of Jesus Christ" (1 Peter 1:6, 7). Satan brings various kinds of "temptations" to believers—not just the enticement to sin, but the trials that wear us down and that make us feel like giving up.

God's intent in allowing these times of testing is not to break us down, but actually the opposite. Notice in each of the above Scriptures that the very thing Satan brings to destroy us is what God intends to make us spiritually strong and radiant with His glory.

ANY TEMPTATION OR ATTACK FROM SATAN MUST PASS GOD'S SCREENING.

"There hath no temptation taken you," the Apostle Paul assures us, "but such as is common to man: but God is faithful, who will not suffer you to be tempted above that ye are able; but will with the temptation also make a way to escape, that ye may be able to bear it" (1 Corinthians 10:13). Paul did not write this as a lofty theological ideal, but as a practical, living reality. Paul himself went through trials so severe that at times he even despaired of life. He understood trials first-hand.

In his experiences with hardship, Paul also learned to know certain important truths: God is faithful! He always keeps His Word. He always cares for His own. He never allows Satan free rein with believers. As in the case of Job, God said to Satan, "You may go so far and no further. Take his possessions, but don't touch him." And later, "You may touch his body, but do not take his life."

In Paul's own life, the "messenger of Satan to buffet" could do only so much. In response to Paul's pleading, God answered, "My grace is sufficient for thee: for my strength is made perfect in weakness" (2 Corinthians 12:9). Paul came to such trust in the faithfulness of God and in the grace of God, that he said, in effect, "Bring it on." Paul knew that God would never allow Satan to do anything that was beyond his ability, through God's enabling grace, to withstand.

WHATEVER SATAN DOES TO BELIEVERS IS FROM WITHOUT AS AN ATTACKER, NOT FROM WITHIN AS A RESIDENT.

The realm of evil spirits and how they affect believers is

often attended with misunderstanding and confusion. Some believers attempt to deal with particularly difficult sins—such as lust, addictions, anger, or pride—as "spirits" of lust, anger, etc. That is, they believe an evil spirit of lust has gained a "stronghold" in a believer's life and must be cast out in the name of Jesus.

In a realm we cannot see, we must beware of speculation. When we hear teaching on this subject, we are wise to ask careful questions: What does the Bible say? How did Jesus and the apostles address these issues? Is there Scriptural precedent for what is being taught? We must also beware of the dangers that come from too much focus on demonic forces.

When Jesus first gave His disciples power over the enemy, they came back rejoicing, "Lord, even the devils are subject unto us through thy name!" (Luke 10:17). Jesus replied, "I beheld Satan as lightning fall from heaven. Behold, I give unto you power to tread on serpents and scorpions, and over all the power of the enemy: and nothing shall by any means hurt you. Notwithstanding in this rejoice not, that the spirits are subject unto you; but rather rejoice, because your names are written in heaven" (vv. 18-20). A focus on casting out demons can make us heady. It can divert us from what is more important to what is less important. It can give the enemy more publicity and attention than is healthy, even if it is negative.

The New Testament does not give us magic formulas either for discerning evil spirits or for casting them out. But as we study the example and teaching of both Jesus and the apostles, a number of things become clear to us:

1. *People can be demon-possessed.* That is, they can so open themselves to Satan that they come under his ownership and power. In such a condition, they may do and say things that are not of themselves, but are

done supernaturally by the demon speaking and acting through their bodies.

2. *The person possessed by an evil spirit is helpless in himself to find deliverance.* He cannot break the hold the
evil spirit has on him.

3. *Sin gives access to the devil.* Certain kinds of sin in particular seem to give Satan access—using demonic pow-
ers or involving oneself in occult activities, for example,
opens the door for demons to invade our lives.

4. *Jesus has power over the enemy.* He demonstrated this
over and over during His ministry, and in His resurrection
He was placed "far above all principality, and power,
and might, and dominion, and every name that is
named, not only in this world, but also in that which is
to come" (Ephesians 1:21). No evil power can resist Him,
and those who call on His name in faith can find deliverance from any evil spirit.

5. *Those who believe in Jesus experience the living Christ
in their hearts, and the evil one cannot harm them.* "We
know that anyone born of God does not continue to
sin; the one who was born of God keeps him safe, and
the evil one does not touch him" (1 John 5:18, NIV).[1] The
teaching and example of the New Testament is con-
sistent and clear: those who are "in Christ" have Christ
living in them. Satan and his demons tempt, attack, hin-
der, and harass from without, not as residents within.

To attempt to deal with deeply rooted sin, therefore, we
must be wise and balanced. On the one hand, we must not
deny the reality of the devil or his ability to ensnare people in
sin, and, on the other hand, we must not see casting out
demons as a quick fix to habitual sin. Steve Gallagher, in his

book, *At the Altar of Sexual Idolatry*, speaks of this need for balance:

> Many who operate in the area of deliverance greatly overemphasize the role demons play in habitual sin. They seem to be looking for an easy answer, or perhaps they are simply enthralled with the idea of ordering demons around.
>
> At the opposite end of the spectrum are those who claim all of a person's problems can be attributed only to himself. This is equally wrong. The idea of there being demonic forces at work in this world is a concept they prefer not to think about.[2]

The enemy is real. He uses a variety of methods to get believers to fall, including enticement to sin and harassment with hardship. Believers know God is faithful. He will not allow temptations or testing above what we are able to bear. God always has purposes in what He allows in our lives, and when we go to Him for help, we have the assurance that His grace will be enough for whatever we face.

FOR FURTHER STUDY:

1. What trials in your life have been especially hard for you to face?
2. How have you been tempted in those trials?
3. What truths are important for you to keep in focus in order to resist those temptations?
4. In your own words, describe the role of the devil in the temptation of believers.
5. Read the following verses, and list the things you learn about temptation, the devil, or deliverance.

a. Matthew 12:42-45
b. Matthew 17:14-21
c. Luke 22:31, 32
d. 1 Thessalonians 2:18
e. 2 Timothy 2:26
f. Hebrews 2:14
g. 1 John 4:4

2

Understanding Sexual Temptation

"Men do not despise a thief,
if he steal to satisfy his soul
when he is hungry;
but whoso committeth adultery
with a woman lacketh understanding:
he that doeth it destroyeth his own soul.
A wound and dishonour shall he get;
and his reproach shall not be wiped away."
Proverbs 6:30, 32, 33

All sin is wrong. But as the above verses imply, some sins are attended with greater consequences than others. In this chapter we want to explore more specifically the nature of sexual sin and the temptations that surround it. The Book of Proverbs abounds with guidelines, warnings, and maxims about sexual temptation. This tells us not only that there are many dangers in this area of our lives, but also that it has been a problem through the centuries.

SEXUAL PASSION IS A VERY POWERFUL HUMAN DRIVE.

Although Sigmund Freud was wrong to believe that the sexual drive was the root motivation for human behavior and thought, his theory had enough truth to make it believable and popular for a time. Sexual urges are strong. They have been compared to wild horses (that need to be tamed), to fire (that can quickly sweep out of control), to high-voltage electricity, and to many other powerful forces.

Like all things powerful, sexual passion has great potential for good; but when used wrongly or when out of control, it has potential to destroy as well.

Learning to control our sexual urges is an important part of maturity. Control is not stifling the desire or denying that it exists, but requiring it to operate according to the guidelines God has given to safeguard and preserve it for its intended use. This includes the following:

1. Recognizing sexual urges and desires as part of God's design for us.
2. Thanking God that He made us sexual beings.
3. Learning to view members of the opposite sex as whole beings, not simply seeing them and evaluating them according to their sexual appeal.
4. Being committed to preserving one's sexuality for God's purposes alone—as an expression of marital love and commitment.
5. Refusing all urgings to satisfy this powerful drive in wrong ways.
6. Setting up clear safeguards against sin and against specific avenues of temptation.

Learning to control this powerful desire before marriage

is an important step in managing it wisely in marriage. Getting married is not an invitation to turn loose all sexual passion. For sex to be an expression of love, it needs to be channeled—it needs to be restrained, guided, and properly focused.

Typically, learning to control sexual desire is a process. We must deal not only with the strong desire within, but also with the constant urgings of an immoral culture without. Immodesty, flirting, lewd joking, cheating on spouses, and titillating songs, movies, and literature are all part of our culture. These things press upon young men and young women continually, urging them to gratify their sexual desires contrary to God's guidelines. Developing moral strength and integrity includes learning to avoid places of temptation, clarifying one's commitment to moral purity, and ordering relationships in healthy ways.

WHEN SEXUAL PASSION IS UNCONTROLLED, IT BECOMES PERVERTED.

In Chapter 1 we saw that desires in their root sense are good. So it is with the sexual desire. But this is not to say that anything one desires sexually is right and good, and it is particularly not so when one's sexual passions have been inflamed by wrong use.

When a person tries to satisfy the soul's innermost longing for God with something tangible—money, possessions, food or drink, etc.—his soul actually becomes hungrier. So it is with sexual passion. The more one feeds it with illicit pleasure, the stronger it gets, and the more it seeks the forbidden. The married man who turns to pornography stirs his passion to higher levels, even while becoming less satisfied sexually. The heightened desire and the emptied heart push him to seek more thrills—to move from fantasy women to real women. But this too is illicit. And his frustrations along the way urge him to try new avenues.

"Mortify therefore your members which are upon the earth; fornication, uncleanness, inordinate affection, evil concupiscence, and covetousness, which is idolatry" (Colossians 3:5). The Greek word *pathos*, translated "inordinate affection" in this verse, captures this concept of inflamed desire—that is, natural desire gone unnatural by improper stimulation. When God's guidelines for sexual passion are ignored, we cannot say that the desire remains pure. It becomes perverted—it seeks the forbidden above the legitimate. Perverted desire not only finds expression in what is wrong, but it becomes essentially wrong.

The Apostle Paul describes this even more forcefully in Romans 1. "Wherefore God also gave them up to uncleanness through the lusts of their own hearts, to dishonour their own bodies between themselves: for this cause God gave them up unto vile affections: for even their women did change the natural use into that which is against nature: and likewise also the men, leaving the natural use of the woman, burned in their lust one toward another; men with men working that which is unseemly, and receiving in themselves that recompence of their error which was meet," or as the NIV says, "received in themselves the due penalty for their perversion" (Romans 1:24, 26, 27).

God designed the sexual relationship to be a powerful bonding experience in marriage—a deep expression of lifelong love and commitment between a husband and wife. Its strongly sensual nature offers a sensory and tangible expression of the intangible. When this powerful desire is satisfied wrongly, it becomes corrupted. That which is natural becomes unnatural. That which was intended to be wholesome and right becomes unhealthy and wrong.

WHEN SEXUAL PASSION IS GIVEN FREE REIGN, IT RUINS RELATIONSHIPS.

When sex becomes an end in itself instead of an expression of love, it turns selfish in nature and resists restraints. This unrestrained sexual desire does not grow out of a relationship or seek to express commitment in a relationship. Turned loose simply to find sensual pleasure, it may actually avoid relationships.

The man simply seeking sexual pleasure, in other words, is thinking of himself and of gratifying his desire. He thinks of "us" primarily as a means of satisfying "me." He desires a woman, not a wife. And because a real woman is seldom content to be used selfishly, and because a real woman would actually refuse to live solely (or even primarily) for his sexual pleasure, he easily turns to a fantasy woman rather than a real woman. In his mind, she exists for him—this fantasy woman is willing to do whatever, whenever, and however. No real woman could be like this. In reality, she could be much more to him because life and relationship and marriage are far more than sex. But as his life comes to revolve around sex, he not only misses the "much more" of life, but also destroys the true meaning (and rich essence) of sexual fulfillment as well.

The result is that the more selfish and unrestrained a person's sexual passions become, the less able the person is to establish and maintain real relationships. He creates in his mind an image no real person could be, and consciously or subconsciously pushes the real people in his life toward that unreal image. That pressure destroys relationships. In his mind, the relationship exists to serve the sexual passion, which is contrary to God's design—that sexual passion is to be an expression of love and commitment.

The same is true for a woman, of course, who spends her

time fantasizing about men. As she lives in the realm of her imaginations about a man—or the imaginations provided by her favorite soap opera or romance novel—she creates a mental image no real man could live up to.

FOR FURTHER STUDY:

1. "Sexual desire is right and good." Tell how this statement is understood correctly and how it may be understood incorrectly.
2. Based on Romans 1:18 ff, list some results of indulging sexual passions without restraint.
3. According to Colossians 3:5, with what measures are we to deal with inflamed sexual desires? What do these severe measures tell us about these desires?
4. Give examples of how a person pursuing sex as an end in itself may actually avoid relationships. What long-term effects would this bring about?
5. In what ways can a real woman not live up to a fantasy woman? In what ways can a fantasy woman not measure up to a real woman?
6. In what ways can a real man not live up to a fantasy man? In what ways can a fantasy man not measure up to a real man?
7. How does the practice of sexual fantasizing affect the character of a man or a woman?

SEXUAL TEMPTATION IS ANY URGING TO SATISFY SEXUAL DESIRE CONTRARY TO GOD'S GUIDELINES.

As we have seen, God designed sex as an expression of marital love. Temptation is enticement to satisfy sexual desire

otherwise. This would include:
- Any kind of sexual relations outside of marriage.
- Fantasizing about sexual relations outside of marriage.
- Using another person for sexual arousal, even when it does not lead to sexual relations.
- Attempting to stir sexual desire in another person. (Provocative dress is not simply a "man's problem." The woman who wears low necklines, short skirts, slit clothing, and the like is inviting men to sin with their eyes and minds even if she denies them sexual pleasures directly with her body.)
- Invading the privacy of another either visually or by touch.
- Reading about (or watching) the sexual adventures of others.
- Playing on sexual desire to promote or to sell something else. The advertising world is brazenly deceitful here.

These and other temptations to stir or satisfy sexual desires are rampant in our society. But they are not new. Paul wrote to the new believers in Thessalonica, "For this is the will of God, even your sanctification, that ye should abstain from fornication: that every one of you should know how to possess his vessel in sanctification and honour; not in the lust of concupiscence, even as the Gentiles which know not God" (1 Thessalonians 4:3-5). Sexual sins are a problem in every society, and every society has some sort of laws to try to govern this powerful drive. Furthermore, wherever those laws exist, men and women look for ways to get around the restrictions.

As we have seen, God has specific guidelines for the exercise and fulfillment of sexual desire. Thus, God is not against sexual expression. He designed the sexual relationship to be a powerful cohesive force in marriage. But leading off from the straight road of sexual purity are a thousand byways to illegitimate pleasure.

Satan would have us believe we are depriving ourselves if we adhere to God's standards. He paints the good path as boring and uninviting, and he lights the paths into sexual sin with dazzling displays, filled with intoxicating pleasures. As the Proverbs writer says, those who listen to these lies do not know that their steps lead to destruction and death. "He goeth after her straightway, as an ox goeth to the slaughter, or as a fool to the correction of the stocks; till a dart strike through his liver; as a bird hasteth to the snare, and knoweth not that it is for his life. Her house is the way to hell, going down to the chambers of death" (Proverbs 7:22, 23, 27).

FOR FURTHER STUDY:

1. In what ways are God's guidelines for our sexuality the same for both men and women?

2. Give examples of guidelines that seem to be gender-specific. What do these differences suggest about men and women?

3. Are there ways these gender-specific guidelines might be (or have been) used to create a double standard?

4. How did Judah follow a double standard in Genesis 38:12-26? Do you think there are similar problems in our culture?

5. Consider this contradiction in our culture: Ladies dress in ways that draw the attention of men to their bodies; yet ladies deny that their appearance is provocative, or they say that if they are stirring lust in men, it is the man's problem. What accounts for this contradiction?

SEXUAL SINS CALL FOR COVER.

All sin begs for cover. This is the nature of sin—it cannot stand light, despises exposure, looks for any excuse to justify itself. Jesus said, "For every one that doeth evil hateth the light, neither cometh to the light, lest his deeds should be reproved" (John 3:20). But sexual sin in particular, because it is attended with much shame, finds countless covers in order to appear legitimate.

Those who yield to sexual sin do so by embracing lies—believing ideas that simply are not true. And then they resort to further distorting reality—in their own minds and in the minds of others—so that they can live with the guilt of sexual sin. Following is a partial list of ways sexual sinners try to hide their sins:

1. *They use terms that make it seem harmless.* For example, they call it "play" or "messing around," or they say they were just "checking things out" or they were "playing doctor."

2. *They project the blame for their actions on others.* They say "she asked for it" or "she liked it." Or they say that by her actions or manners she was asking for it. Some men blame their sexual sins on their wives—because their wives are cold or don't cooperate with their sexual desires, they have to get it somewhere else.

3. *They rationalize.* That is, they find "reasons" that seem to justify their sin. A husband, for example, may say of masturbation, "Well, it's better than adultery." Or a man may say that he looks at pornography because he is doing a study and wants to keep abreast of what's current. A pornographer may reason that looking at other women makes him better able to please his wife, or a woman may use similar reasoning to justify

reading romance literature. A man may say he is simply "oversexed," which in his mind means he is less responsible for sexual sins than other men.

4. *They compensate for their guilt by being nice, generous, or very "righteous."* The front others see is kind and considerate. It may show a ready smile and be willing to "do anything for others." Or the front may wear a righteous face, being excessively "conservative" or strict about home rules or church rules. The righteous front keeps others from seeing (or even suspecting) the dirty interior.

5. *They hide it or its consequences under a cloak of forgiveness.* That is, they may easily say "I'm sorry," and then demand that forgiveness means this is behind them and no one may refer to it again. They may even accuse people of not forgiving when those whom they have used in their sin need to work through the consequences.

6. *They blame God.* They ask questions such as, "Why did God even allow me to see that advertisement?" Or, "Why did God make us with such strong urges?" Or "Why did He let me make that phone call?"

But the bottom line is that to live with the shame of sexual sin, men and women learn to distort reality. They develop habits of misrepresenting, mislabeling, minimizing, exaggerating, blaming, telling only part of the story, putting on a front, or outright lying about their activities so they can live with their sin.

Habits of dishonesty become deeply ingrained in a person who lives in sexual sin. And they spread to other areas of life as well.

In the Bible we have the account of Samson, a man who had a fatal attraction to Philistine women. Samson was also a deceiver, a manipulator, and a liar. He hid his plans from his parents, used deception in his dealings with the Philistines, and outright lied to the women in his life. Ironically, Samson was caught through the intrigue of a deceitful woman, even while he was playing with the fire of sexual sin.

Habits of deception almost always accompany patterns of immorality. In the church this is especially tragic. God's people are called out of sin. It is expected that they live holy lives and demonstrate trustworthiness. Some who live in sexual sin purposely use the front of godliness to cover their sin.

In *The Scarlet Letter,* Nathaniel Hawthorne tells the story of a pastor who had committed adultery with a woman in his community. Living under the weight of his guilt, the pastor preached with such self-abasement that the people interpreted it as deep humility. And the more they admired him for his holiness, the deeper became his shame for his sin.

All covers for sin are wrong, but it seems that using the cover of "righteousness" for sin is especially odious in the sight of God and man. A man who hides a life of pornography behind the cover of being a wonderful Sunday school teacher; a priest who uses his position to gain sexual favors from altar boys; a father who describes his fondling of his daughter as his duty to teach her about her sexuality or his way of meeting her needs; a man who covers a habit of internet porn with a goodhearted front, who will do "anything for anyone"—all these are covers with frightful costs. First, there is the cost to the name of God and the reputation of His people. Then there is the cost to one's family and relationships. And finally, there is the cost to one's own soul—*covered sin is devastating to one's character.* To onlookers, using righteousness as a deceptive cover for sexual sin increases the ugliness of this sin. And ironically, the very awareness of how people view this hypocrisy fuels the deceptive habits of "righteous" sexual offenders. Covering can become such a way of life that finally, even the offender does not always know when he is real and when he is pretending.

SEXUAL TEMPTATION AND SEXUAL DESIRE ARE OFTEN HIDDEN BEHIND LEGITIMATE ACTIVITIES.

We have already discussed this to some extent in exploring how a person uses a "righteous" cover for sexual sin. But there are many more ways illegitimate sexual desires are hidden behind legitimate activities.

A man and woman may find themselves drawn to each other, may begin to open their hearts to each other, may even feel the urgings of desire for one another, and may declare that their relationship is "just friends." This is an especially attractive cover when both they and others know a special relationship would be wrong (for example, if one or both are married to someone else or if they are closely related to each other). They cannot afford to be honest about deeper attractions, so they find a "legitimate" reason for the time they spend together.

A boss may spend time with his secretary "to keep up with the business" but be driven with an underlying desire for more time with her. Or he may lean close to her "to examine something on her desk" when in reality, he is being urged by his desire for physical closeness.

Couples may spend time together "because we are such good friends" when secretly, they are attracted to one another's spouses.

A pastor may stop in at a home "to visit," or he may spend

time talking with ladies "because he cares about them." But he is gratified when they open their hearts and lives to him, by being able to draw out their hearts, and by the emotional closeness he has with them. And for both of them, this emotional closeness may eventually be the route to physical closeness—a touch, a hug, and finally more.

Men and women may hug one another in extended family relationships or in the "close fellowship" of a brotherhood and declare it is "just family" or "just like family." But their underlying drive is actually sensual.

Or a man may begin to treat (and talk about) a younger woman as "my little sister," and she may begin to refer to him as "my big brother" when in reality, they are feeding their desire for emotional intimacy, and ultimately for more.

Now the reality is that these kinds of activities and relationships have legitimate places in our lives. A boss may need to work on a problem with his secretary's help. Couples may be good friends and spend time together. Pastors do need to be involved with the members of their church. It is right to show affection in a family and compassion in the church. And sometimes someone outside of the family does fill a place similar to a family member.

The effectiveness of the cover is exactly in its legitimacy. The point is that these activities and relationships may be used as a cover for sexual desire. We would be wrong to throw out all friendship, closeness, and caring because there is danger of using them as covers for satisfying sensual desires. But we must beware of both the power of our sexual passion and the potential we have for hiding it.

When someone declares, "We're just friends," or "He's like a big brother to me," it should raise caution flags. Typically, when the relationship is healthy, no one needs to give it legitimacy. These explanations are especially alarming when they are given to explain liberties that overstep proper boundaries: touch, for example (especially teasing touch), or frequent and extended time spent together, or extended phone calls.

If sexual desire is the hidden drive behind seemingly innocent activities, it will eventually be revealed. Suddenly the teasing touch or the intimate sharing can no longer hide the underlying drive. Alone and looking into one another's eyes, the real motivations are unmasked. Many have fallen at that point. The desire has been fanned, sometimes so secretly that the person is unaware himself, but fanned nonetheless. And when the heightened desire is mutually acknowledged, it may well be too strong to resist.

Another twist to the problem of hiding illegitimate desires behind legitimate activities is that this may be happening for one person, but not for the other. A secretary may be totally innocent in helping her boss with a work problem, while the boss uses the problem as a mask to feed his desires. Or the reverse may be true—the wrong motives may lie on the part of the secretary, while the boss is sincere. A pastor may have righteous intentions in helping a distressed lady in his congregation, but she may be using the distress, even creating it, to gain his attention. Again, the point is that we must be aware of the power of this drive and of its tendency to hide.

FOR FURTHER STUDY:

1. List the six ways people hide their sexual sins. Of the six, which seems most commonly used in your observation?

2. Can you find Biblical examples of people using these tactics to cover their sin (not just sexual sin)?

3. Make a list of legitimate activities behind which people

hide their sexual desires.

4. Do you think men, or women, tend to be quicker to be dishonest about their true desires? Explain your answer.

5. Choose one of the following passages and make a list of the deceptions you see in the thinking of the person guilty of sexual sin: a. David, 2 Samuel 11. b. Amnon, 2 Samuel 13:1-20.

6. Now take this list of deceptions, and write out what is true.

7. What concerns do you have about potential screens (for sexual desires) among the people you interact with?

8. What kinds of safeguards might help avoid these hazards?

9. Is it possible to overemphasize safeguards against improper sexual behavior? And if so, what are the effects of that overemphasis?

10. When a person uses his or her position (such as a pastor or teacher) as a righteous cover for sexual sin, what adverse effects are there on the name of God and the work of God?

SEXUAL SIN IS ATTENDED WITH A GREAT DEGREE OF SHAME.

In the verses at the beginning of this chapter, the proverb compared sexual sin with stealing. Both are sin. Both should be viewed as wrong. But while one can sometimes see a "justifiable reason" for stealing (when a man is hungry, for example), we seldom justify sexual sin. We view the sexual transgressor as wrong. And note that this passage is not saying that stealing is sometimes justifiable—only that in our mind's eye we can see a "reason" for doing it. But a man will search in vain for such a reason when his wife has been violated by another man. No explanation is reasonable.

And although, because of the grace of God, sexual sins can be forgiven, this passage indicates they are not forgotten. "A wound and dishonour shall he get; and his reproach shall not be wiped away" (Proverbs 6:33).

There is probably no human relationship that touches us as powerfully as the sexual relationship. And sexual transgression therefore seems to leave the most indelible impression on our minds. We see this reality reflected in various ways: in the difficulty people have forgiving sexual sins, in the attention the media gives to the sexual transgressions of leaders, in the rapid spread of rumors about this kind of sin, and in the regular attention given to the whole subject of sex in our culture. We see it even in the criminal world, where child molesters and rapists are lowest on the totem pole of criminals. This is a subject that catches our attention. This is a sin that is attended with special shame.

SEXUAL TEMPTATION IS TIED TO DEEPER DESIRES.

We noted that this can be so with other physical desires as well. For example, Satan tempted Jesus, "If thou be the Son of God, command that these stones be made bread" (Matthew 4:3). That is, Jesus was tempted to eat not simply to satisfy His need for food, but in order to prove He was God's Son.

With sexual temptation, however, underlying desires are even more significant. For a man, the sexual relationship validates his manhood—he is here demonstrating his male power, pouring out his male energy, expressing himself as a hunter and conqueror and leader all in one. For a woman, the sexual relationship validates her womanhood—she is experiencing the fulfillment of her attractive power in its highest form, drawing her man to herself, being possessed by powerful, encircling love.

The sexual experience, then, involves more than pleasure. It is an expression of manhood and womanhood. It is a way of possessing and of being possessed. It is a deep seeking and an intimate experience of being found.

This is the reason God intended the sexual relationship to be the expression of love in a lifelong commitment. The husband is not merely validating "a woman" as a sexual being, but he is validating a woman he discovers intimately and affirms as his own; and he is validating himself as the one who has discovered her and pledges to be her protector and provider, the one she may claim as her own.

The desire to know and be known by another human being is most tangibly experienced in sexual union. "Adam knew Eve his wife; and she conceived" (Genesis 4:1). Sex is a baring of the heart, an opening up, an invitation to be known and embraced at the deepest level of human interaction.

Sex, therefore, is inseparably tied to who we are. This has many implications both in right and wrong sexual experience. In the next chapter, we will explore these implications in more detail, but we lay the foundation here. When either a man or a woman's identity has been marred by abuse, neglect, or serious distortions of role models, especially in the formative stages of life, he/she typically has difficulties with healthy sexual relations.

A man with a distorted manhood may seek to conquer simply to validate himself. He may avoid letting himself really be known. He may fear intimacy. He may reject intimacy with females altogether. He may seek sex in ways that purposely avoid commitment.

A woman with a distorted womanhood, on the other hand, may seek the attentions of men simply to validate herself, to give her a sense of control as a woman. She, too, may fear intimacy even while she craves it. She may seek physical intimacy, but avoid emotional closeness. Or she may seek emotional closeness through physical intimacy.

When real life seems dangerous, when making oneself known to another in the context of commitment seems scary—either because one may be rejected or because one may not be able to live up to a partner's expectations—it seems easy to resort to alternatives. Men may turn to pornography. Women may turn to romance stories (in books, magazines, videos, or TV soap operas). In either case, the issue of who they are (or more accurately, who they aren't) seems, on the surface, to be resolved. The man can imagine himself to be fully accepted by the voluptuous woman on the page; who he is in real life is superseded by the fantasy of who "she" makes him to be in his imagination. Likewise, the woman in the romance story is pursued, swept off her feet, loved, even heartbroken, in ways that affirm her as a woman, regardless of who she is in real life.

As we noted earlier, this doesn't result in fulfillment. In fact, the more a person lives in fantasy, the less equipped he is to face the real world. Real men and real women aren't able to fill the distorted desires and expectations of the fantasy world, and the men and women who live in fantasy not only deepen their disappointment in those around them, but correspondingly deepen their disappointment in themselves.

Who we are and who we aren't are major issues in sexual temptation. In the next chapter, we will explore more fully the implications of these underlying issues.

FOR FURTHER STUDY:

1. What evidences in our culture demonstrate the high degree of shame attending sexual sin?

2. How does the sexual relationship validate manhood? How does the sexual relationship validate womanhood?

3. How do men use sex wrongly to validate themselves? How do women use sex wrongly to validate themselves?

4. What are the effects of sexual fantasy on actual relationships?

5. List any ways you have lived in a fantasy sexual world, and describe the extent of that involvement.

6. If your involvements in fantasy have been extensive or ongoing, take some time to pray, asking God to help you to be honest and accurate.

    a. Tell how your fantasizing makes you feel about yourself.

    b. Describe your biggest fear/struggle in actual relationships.

    c. Identify the false expectations your fantasizing has created for you.

    d. With a trusted parent or pastor, bring these needs to the Lord and pray for cleansing and a change of life.

Note: A more thorough guide for cleansing the heart is given in Appendix A. If you have struggled with bondage to sexual sins, consider the suggestions given there.

3

IDENTIFYING
UNDERLYING ISSUES

"The woman saith unto him,
Sir, give me this water, that I thirst not, . . .
Jesus saith unto her,
Go, call thy husband, and come hither.
The woman answered and said,
I have no husband.
Jesus said unto her, Thou hast well said,
I have no husband:
For thou hast had five husbands;
and he whom thou now hast
is not thy husband."
John 4:15-18

Sexual sin is a problem in itself. It calls for repentance, a cleansing of the heart, and a change of living. But sexual sin is not always a problem by itself. Sometimes it is quite superficial on the overall landscape of the soul. Other problems not only lie deeper but also function as major contributors to the sexual sins. And until we understand and deal with those underlying problems, our efforts to deal with the sexual sins are in vain.

In this chapter we wish to explore some of the underlying issues that make people vulnerable to sexual sin.

SEXUAL PROMISCUITY MAY REFLECT EMPTINESS.

In John 4, we have the account of Jesus talking with the Samaritan woman. With a few simple questions and statements, Jesus led this lady to an underlying issue in her sexual promiscuity. She had had five husbands. The one she now lived with was not her husband. How many other relationships had she had? We do not know. But she was a woman with an inner thirst, and the multiple men in her life had not satisfied her. She lived on empty.

The glaring problems in the woman's life were relational. She went from one man to another. But the underlying problem was a hunger that had never been satisfied. Furthermore, her method of trying to satisfy that hunger only left her emptier. She was not a satisfied woman. She did not have contentment in her heart.

While emptiness always results from sexual promiscuity, it can also be a cause. That is, when a person does not have healthy relationships, or when he or she lives with no close relationships, particularly when primary relationships such as family relationships are empty and meaningless, relational hunger increases. Like hunger and thirst, the desire for close, secure relationships is a part of our makeup. A child who grows up in an emotional desert is susceptible to the temptation to seek relationships indiscriminately. And like the woman at the well, that child may learn to connect in superficial ways and avoid meaningful relationships.

THE PLACE OF A FATHER.

Over and over, studies have shown that children who are not closely connected with their parents demonstrate behavioral problems.[1] They seek attention wrongly. They do not adjust well to new situations. They easily get into trouble.

The father especially plays an important role in the spiritual and moral development of children.

In the Bible, we have the tragic story of Absalom. We often focus on Absalom's rebellion. And it deserves our attention. But Absalom's uprising was preceded by two years of receiving a cold shoulder from his father, David (2 Samuel 14:28). And Absalom consummated the overthrow of the kingdom by engaging in open sex with ten of David's servant wives (2 Samuel 16:22).

This does not excuse Absalom's sin. He was responsible for his own actions, and he died for his sins. But the emotional distance on David's part was surely a contributing factor in Absalom's sexual sins. The simple reality is that young men need a close relationship with their fathers and distance makes them morally vulnerable.

Women also need close relationship with their fathers. Almost invariably I have found that ladies who struggle with masturbation have had a poor relationship with their father, or they have significant longings for a deeper relationship. In this observation, it is important to note that the relationship does not need to be abusive to create difficulty for the daughter. Some fathers assume that if they are not overtly hurtful, they have a good relationship with their daughters. This is simply not so. A daughter wants her father to be actively involved in her life.

I remember well the shock and hurt on the faces of a Christian couple when they learned that their teenage daughter had had sexual relationships with several men. "What we don't understand," they said in bewilderment, "is that we have had such good times with our daughter. We have lots of fun together."

When I talked to the daughter, however, she said, "Oh, sure, we can have fun together. But if I have something I'm struggling with, I would never go to my parents about it." The absence of conflict, even the presence of fun, did not take away the yearning she had for parents who took the time to know her and who provided opportunities to talk about deeper things that mattered to her.

In the Book of Esther, we have a beautiful example of a girl's emptiness filled in a healthy way. Esther had neither father nor mother. But her cousin Mordecai "took her for his own daughter" (Esther 2:7). The relationship was so close that even after Esther was given to the king, she "did the commandment of Mordecai, like as when she was brought up with him" (2:20). Mordecai was very involved in Esther's life, providing a sense of guidance, protection, and safety that kept her pure and upright even when she was living in a heathen king's harem.

We obviously do not know the details of the Samaritan woman's relationship with her father. But she certainly did not know how to live in healthy closeness with the men in her life. And it would not be imagining too much to assume that her relationship to her father was nothing like Mordecai's close relationship with Esther.

And so, although we must not automatically attribute

sexual sins on the part of either man or woman to a vacancy in their relationship with their father, we must on the other hand, recognize that the absent or uninvolved father in many homes today is a powerful contributing factor to the promiscuity in our culture. Ours is a culture of emptiness. And ours is a culture of sexual promiscuity. The two characteristics are closely related. For example, one survey found that 80% of convicted rapists grew up in fatherless homes.

Adolescents need all the help they can get to navigate their way through the minefields of sexual sin in our day. A close relationship with a morally pure, spiritually stable father is not a guarantee they will make it safely, but such a relationship certainly provides a strong protection against sexual sin.

Besides establishing a close relationship with their children, fathers and mothers need to be morally upright themselves. Over and over in the Bible we have the command for parents to train their children in God's ways. And the fundamental principle of training is that we train best by our own lives. Children follow who we are more consistently than they follow what we say. Moral purity in parents is a powerful call to children to live morally upright lives.

The opposite is also true. When a father is impure, he increases the likelihood of sexual sins in his children. Probably the most wicked woman described in the Bible is Jezebel, a woman known for her painted face and styled hair (2 Kings 9:30) and associated with a sexually loose lifestyle (Revelation 2:20). Her forefathers were Baal worshipers, a religion so morally corrupt it is a shame even to speak of the details, but "worship" involved sexual relations with temple prostitutes both male and female. And through Jezebel's influence (see 1 Kings 21:25), Ahab "did very abominably in following idols, according to all things as did the Amorites" (v. 26). It is understandable, then, that when their son Ahaziah took the throne, "he did evil in the sight of the LORD, and walked in the way of his father, and in the way of his mother" (1 Kings 22:52).

Only the grace of God can break such a legacy of sin. Again, we want to clarify that the influence of fathers and mothers is not deterministic—by calling on the Lord, a son or daughter can reverse an immoral legacy. Furthermore, an immoral son or daughter is still personally responsible for his or her sin. But the point remains: the lifestyle of parents is powerfully influential in the choices of their children.

FOR FURTHER STUDY:

1. What do you think the woman at the well was thirsty for?

2. What do you think Absalom wanted from his father?

3. What are the most significant ways fathers in our culture are not meeting the needs of their children?

4. Think about ways fathers in Christian homes are not meeting their children's needs. Are your answers any different from those for Question #3?

5. Are there ways others can step in to fill empty areas in the lives of young people? Are there ways it may be inappropriate to try to meet those needs?

6. What do you think are the results of a young person carrying empty spots (from the parent-child relationship) into his marriage?

7. Describe any empty areas you may have struggled with in your own life, and tell how that emptiness has driven you.

SEXUAL PROBLEMS ARE SOMETIMES FED BY REBELLION.

We looked at the example of Absalom and noticed the vacuum in his relationship with his father David. We also saw how that vacuum contributed to both rebellion and sexual sin. What we want to explore here is the observation that rebellion can be an underlying factor in sexual sin.

Eli the priest neglected to restrain his sons. They ate what they wanted to eat and when and how, and no one dared stand in their way. Eli did object, but he clearly did not take the measures he should have. His boys rebelled against him and against God because from Eli, at least, there were no consequences. God said to Eli, "Wherefore kick ye at my sacrifice and at mine offering, which I have commanded in my habitation; and honourest thy sons above me, to make yourselves fat with the chiefest of all the offerings of Israel my people?" (1 Samuel 2:29). But now notice that these young rebels not only had an unrestrained appetite for food, but they also "lay with the women that assembled at the door of the tabernacle" (1 Samuel 2:22).

Here we see the link between rebellion and sexual sin. The same spirit in a young man or woman that throws off authority easily throws off other restraints. The attitude that says, "Don't tell me what to do," sets a person up to do what pleases the flesh, which actually undermines his moral strength. Even when he knows better, he doesn't have the strength to do better. A rebel reflecting on what he did will sometimes wonder, *Why in the world did I do that? Do I really want to be this kind of person?* But he learns to shrug off those inner objections, especially when he has another run-in with authority.

In the Israelites, we see another example of the link between rebellion and sexual sin. When the people rebelled against

God, they often became sexually promiscuous. At Mt. Sinai, for example, they cast off restraint and threw off their clothes as well (see Exodus 32:25). And the Book of Judges is full of stories showing a direct correlation between rebellion against the Lord and sexual sins.

In our day it is no different. The 1960s were characterized by casting aside rules and indulging in sexual pleasure. Two main themes in the rock music of that era were rebellion and sex. Frank Zappa, from a rock group called "Mothers of Invention" said, "Rock music is sex. The big beat matches the body rhythms." And the Rolling Stones had this to say about rock music and rebellion: "Rock is more than music. It is the energy center of the new culture and youth rebellion."[2]

In spite of those open acknowledgements by rock musicians (and those are only samples of a host of such comments made during that era), many Christians believed—and many today still believe—that such music was harmless and had little to do with the moral deterioration of society. Although our subject is not music, I must mention that youths living in rebellion to their parents are commonly drawn to (even bound to) music that feeds their rebellion.

The reality is that rebels increase their vulnerability to the pull of sexual sin. Because the rebel is out from under the protection of his authority, his "control center" becomes himself. Like the prodigal son, he lives to please self. And sexual sins certainly do give immediate pleasure.

The rebel seldom realizes the tie between his rebellion and his sexual indulgence. He thinks he is having fun and gaining freedom. He does not see that his negative attitudes toward authority figures actually push him toward the forbidden. In his way of thinking, lines are made to walk across, rules are made to be broken. His mockery of authority is commonly rooted in deep anger toward particular authority figures. But he typically covers that anger with gaiety—laughing at sin and laughing at consequences. His plunge into sensuality is often headlong, reckless, and exhilarating.

Fortunately, there are consequences. Money runs out. Relationships crumble. Reproofs come like arrows. Sorrows pound like hail. And the rebel eventually finds himself in a hole he can't climb out of—dirty, destitute, and wondering how he ever got there.

This is the place of redemption for many. They hit bottom hard enough that they look for a way out. Some turn to Christ. Some go back home. Some die. Others can't find their way. They may have burned their bridges so completely that they are too ashamed to turn back. Or they may have no good home or church to which they can return, and they simply don't know where to go.

FOR FURTHER STUDY:

1. Describe in your own words the tie between rebellion and sexual promiscuity.
2. To what extent do you think music has influenced the moral standards of the Western world?
3. Now for you personally, describe as honestly as you can how music has had either positive or negative effects on your moral standards.
4. Has your music resulted in tension in your relationships? If so, tell why you think it has created tension.
5. Describe your relationship with authority figures in your life. Do you see any connection between your relationship with authorities in your life and your moral standards (either positively or negatively)?

6. Read these Scriptures and make a list of wholesome attitudes toward authority: Exodus 20:12; Leviticus 19:32; Proverbs 23:22; 30:17; Romans 13:1-6; 1 Thessalonians 5:12, 13; Hebrews 13:7, 17

7. Which of the attitudes in your list have you struggled with?

SEXUAL PROBLEMS CAN BE FED BY ANGER.

The emptiness and rebellion we have looked at as underlying causes in sexual sin are often accompanied by anger. In Absalom, we see all three. After spending two years back in Jerusalem without being allowed to see his father, and after being ignored by Joab, Absalom finally set Joab's fields on fire. That got Joab's attention. And when Joab came storming over to ask Absalom what he was doing, we can sense the seething feelings in Absalom's reply. He said, "Wherefore am I come from Gesher? It had been good for me to have been there still: now therefore let me see the king's face; and if there be any iniquity in me, let him kill me" (2 Samuel 14:32).

Absalom's anger was the anger of grievance. He felt deeply wronged, and he seemed to have nursed his anger for a long time. That kind of anger makes people vulnerable to sexual sin. It creates intense inner tension. The unresolved grievance is easily used to excuse sexual sin. When Absalom had sexual relations with David's concubines, he may or may not have been aware of the grievances driving him. But there are many men and women today who burn with inner anger and give vent to their anger in sexual release.

Some may do this by masturbation. Some may turn to pornography, not only as a matter of lust, but as a way of venting their anger—I can do whatever I want! And some develop a drive to dominate, seeking to find a vulnerable person to exploit. Rapists are typically angry people, men carrying deep grievances. While they may not be consciously angry at the time, they are driven by feelings deep within them about situations they cannot control and burning grudges from the past. Rape is a way of regaining control. It gives them a satisfaction they feel they are denied in other areas of their life.

This is not to say that a person with unresolved anger will always be immoral. But immorality is one way anger finds expression.

Unfortunately, sexual expression driven by anger only increases the problem. A man who masturbates when he is frustrated with an authority figure is then ashamed and becomes angrier. And his conscience may be even more demanding and "unreasonable" than the authority figure he is struggling with. This becomes a vicious cycle—anger, sexual sin, shame, leading to more anger, more sexual sin, and more shame.

FOR FURTHER STUDY:

1. In your own words describe the "anger of grievance."
2. List the things Absalom may have been angry and bitter about (see 2 Samuel 13-15).
3. Anger of grievance can be difficult to acknowledge. We would rather talk about the grievance than our anger. Why do you think this is so?
4. List some of the grievances you have struggled with.
5. How have you responded to these grievances—that is, do you think they still drive you, and in what ways? Or, if they have not driven you, how do you think you have been able to avoid being driven by them?

6. How does God want us to respond to grievances? (Support your answers with Scripture.)

SEXUAL PROMISCUITY CAN BE FED BY PATTERNS OF DECEPTION.

We observed in the last chapter that a special shame accompanies sexual sin and therefore, sexual sins are often hidden behind legitimate activities. Viewed this way, deceptions are an outgrowth of sexual sin. That is, people who transgress God's laws for their sexuality learn to use covers to avoid acknowledging it as sin. But deception can also work as an underlying factor, feeding sexual sins.

The Bible says Satan sometimes masquerades as an "angel of light," and so it is no surprise that his servants do the same (2 Corinthians 11:13, 14). It is in the nature of sinners to pretend to be something they are not and to hide what they really are. Since we all are sinners, we all have firsthand acquaintance with pretending. We learn to wear masks. And unfortunately, we can grow more proficient with age.

Becoming a Christian—acknowledging that we are sinful and need a Saviour—is a start in the direction of being real with ourselves, with God, and with others. But the battle is not over. What we have learned in sin can be difficult to unlearn. Christians also struggle with being real. Sometimes it seems that those who have "become Christians" have simply discovered a better mask.

The following thoughts are not exhaustive on this subject, nor are they intended to be fodder for dissatisfied or disillusioned or disgruntled souls in the church. Some religious groups are very strict in controlling the conduct, words, and appearance of their members. This external strictness, however, is not always what it appears to be. Onlookers may conclude these strict groups are peaceful, righteous, unworldly Christians (almost other-worldly). And many are sincere.

But in reality, externally strict Christianity, especially when coupled with a lack of spiritual vitality, lacks the power to restrain sensual sins. The Apostle Paul said that a focus on rules such as "touch not; taste not; handle not" have "the appearance of wisdom in self-made religion and self-abasement and severe treatment of the body, but are of no value against fleshly indulgence" (Colossians 2:21, 23, NASB).3 Growing up in a religious setting that emphasizes "Do not!" but lacks the power to restrain the flesh is frustrating to say the least. The sense of condemnation and guilt is over-whelming, and sometimes the hopelessness of the situation seems to impel the transgressor into even more sin. What he doesn't want to do, he seems driven to do. There is incredible misery in the heart of a strictly religious person who is privately immoral.

The Pharisees—known for their external strictness—one day brought to Jesus a woman taken in the act of adultery and asked His verdict. Jesus wisely did not pass judgment on a sinful woman in the presence of unrighteous accusers. Instead He wrote on the ground (perhaps it is as well we do not know what He wrote) and then said, "He that is without sin among you, let him first cast a stone at her" (John 8:7). To what sins was He referring? Why did they leave without another word, "being convicted by their own conscience"? Is it assuming too much to suggest that the sins that sent these men on their way were equal to or greater than her sin?

Where was the man who committed adultery with this woman? How did these men catch this woman? What was their acquaintance with her? We don't know the answers to these questions.

But the truth we are after here is that people who live deceptively, people who wear covers, people who become proficient with masks make themselves vulnerable to sexual temptations. When the mask appears to be righteous and when that righteous mask hides an empty soul, the soul loses its discipline to say no to sexual sin. Rather, it seems sometimes to be compelled to sin, driven by the contradictions between the surface mask and the true substance of the heart and by the resultant inner misery.

The applications of this principle are abundant:

1. A man in church ministry who loses his spiritual fervor is dangerously vulnerable to sensual temptation.

2. Young men or women who grow up in an externally strict but spiritually or emotionally sterile environment are especially vulnerable to such sins as private fantasies, masturbation, incest, and bestiality.

3. Strict religious groups who lose their spiritual vitality abound with sexual sins.

4. Youth groups in churches that emphasize externals and have lost true spirituality indulge in sexually suggestive and even sexually explicit activities (such as "bed courtship").

5. Groups that develop a works-based approach to salvation likewise open the door to sexual sins. Consider the church at Thyatira: Jesus said, "I know thy works, and charity, and service, and faith, and thy patience, and thy works; and the last to be more than the first. Notwithstanding I have a few things against thee, because thou sufferest that woman Jezebel, which calleth herself a prophetess, to teach and to seduce my servants to commit fornication" (Revelation 2:19, 20).

If underlying habits of deception find expression in sexual sin (among other expressions), would not the opposite be true as well? Are not honesty, integrity, and truth of soul fortifications against sexual sin? We can say unequivocally they are. Perhaps there is more protection than we have realized in Paul's instruction to have our "loins girt about with truth" (Ephesians 6:14). We do not want to stretch the analogy beyond what the apostle intended, but in the battle for moral purity, our loins must have no false covers. Truth of being—living a life that is real before God and man—is protection against immorality.

SUMMARY

Sexual sin is a problem in itself. It is devastating and needs to be addressed. But many times it is not a problem by itself. Sexual problems may be the result of (even while they are also the cause of) problems such as emptiness, rebellion, anger, and deception. Sometimes we must identify and correct underlying problems before we can address and change wrong sexual behavior.

FOR FURTHER STUDY:

1. In your own words, describe how deception can be both the result of sexual sins and also an underlying cause.

2. During the time David was hiding his sin (about Bathsheba), how do you think he felt when he went to worship? How might he have acted?

3. What are some results of covering sexual sins by pretending to be righteous? (Consider results in one's

personal life, results in one's interpersonal relationships, and results in one's handling of responsibilities.)

4. How can parents hold their children to standards of behavior and appearance without setting them up to be hypocritical?

5. How does hypocrisy make a person more vulnerable to sin? (Use Scripture to support your answer.)

6. In the last section we noted that habits of pretending can make a person more vulnerable to sins of the flesh. Do you agree or disagree with the following statements?

   a. An open sinner is better off than a secret sinner.

   b. A person who lives behind a front will have lustful motives.

   c. Actors and actresses are more vulnerable to sexual sins because they engage in pretense.

   d. Christians who live out their faith have an obligation to be real.

   e. It is dangerous to be too strict.

   f. Christians can have standards of behavior and appearance without being hypocritical.

7. Of the underlying issues discussed in this chapter, which do you think is the most common problem? Which would you personally struggle with most?

4

REPENTING OF MORAL FAILURE

"Wash me thoroughly from mine iniquity,
and cleanse me from my sin.
For I acknowledge my transgressions:
and my sin is ever before me."
Psalm 51:2, 3

David, like a host of others who have committed sexual sins, tasted the bitter consequences of his sin. He lost sweet fellowship with God. He experienced an ugly stain on his godly reputation. The son he fathered with Bathsheba died. David's oldest son, Amnon, sexually violated Tamar, a beautiful daughter of David. In retaliation, Absalom (full brother to Tamar) killed Amnon. Later, Absalom tried to take over the kingdom, and in the process had sexual relations with some of David's wives in a public area. David paid dearly for his sin.

But David also repented. He begged God for cleansing, and he turned back to a life of moral uprightness. In this chapter, we want to explore the path of repentance. And we can say at the outset that there is cleansing from sexual sin. Praise God! By the grace of God, it is possible to leave the life of sin and break the bondage of wrong sexual habits. David's repentance, recorded in Psalm 51, points the way to spiritual cleansing and deliverance. Let's see what we can learn.

DAVID VIEWED HIS SIN AS FOREMOST AGAINST GOD.

"Against thee, thee only, have I sinned, and done this evil in thy sight" (v. 4). David surely had sinned against Uriah, against Bathsheba, against their family, and against his own family. But above all, David realized he had sinned against God. He had violated the law of God, and he had acted in direct disobedience to the One who had made him and called him and led him and protected him through the years. The realization of what he had done against God smote David with crushing force.

To deal with sin in our lives, we must go before God. We must see our sin in the presence of our Maker and our Redeemer. We must contemplate what our sin means to a God who hates sin and who has clearly told us what is right and what is wrong. We must also understand what sin means to a God who was willing to send His Son to save us from sin and to die a horrible death so we can be forgiven. We must kneel before this God until we lay aside every excuse, every cover, every justification, and our sin stands open and bare before His eyes.

There we can let our hearts break for the ugliness of our sin, for the shame we have brought to His name, and for the damage it has done to the image of God in our own hearts. Like David, our tears must flow first before the Lord.

FOR FURTHER STUDY:

1. What evidences show that David's repentance was genuine?
2. Make a list of the people David sinned against by his adultery and murder.
3. Why do you think he says in Psalm 51 that his sin was "only" against God?
4. As specifically as you can, list the ways David's sin was against God.
5. What is the value of seeing that our sin is against God?
6. What are the results of seeing sin only as against other people?

DAVID REALIZED THE SIN HAD DEFILED HIM, AND HE ASKED FOR CLEANSING.

Sin is morally corrupting. It blackens the heart. It stains the conscience. It stands on one's record like an ugly blot.

We can see the dark side of sin in others far quicker than we can see it in ourselves. And ironically, we can see it in ourselves more clearly when the sin becomes public knowledge. We may justify our sin or even refuse to call it sin as long as no one knows about it. But when others know, suddenly the shamefulness of what we have done hits us with terrible power.

While no one knew, David somehow lived with himself. How smugly, we do not know, although surely sometimes his own psalms must have stuck in his throat. But when his cover was blown, the sinfulness of his adultery, the treachery of his murder, and the wickedness of his cover-up scheme—all this moral filth was almost unbearable to him. Listen to his pleas for cleansing in Psalm 51:

"Blot out my transgressions" (v. 1).

"Wash me thoroughly from mine iniquity" (v. 2).

"Cleanse me from my sin" (v. 2).

"Purge me with hyssop, and I shall be clean" (v. 7).

"Wash me, and I shall be whiter than snow" (v. 7).

"Blot out all mine iniquities" (v. 9).

"Create in me a clean heart" (v. 10).

"Renew a right spirit within me" (v. 10).

"Deliver me from bloodguiltiness" (v. 14).

According to the account in 2 Samuel 12, Nathan assured David immediately that his sin was forgiven. "The LORD also hath put away thy sin" (v. 13). But in the days that followed, David still cried out for cleansing. He knew the sin had defiled his heart, and he knew only the Lord could cleanse his heart.

This does not mean a person must beg and plead for days before God will forgive sin. But true repentance carries a deep sense of sin's defilement and does not allow us to treat it lightly.

Covered sin dangerously dulls our sense of sin's wickedness. We can become so accustomed to covering our sin, minimizing it, calling it by acceptable names, or giving "reasons" for our involvement that we want to rush through repentance. With this mindset, we may avoid looking honestly at the defilement within, and we may resent when others make reference to our sin.

David teaches us that true penitence is coupled with a full awareness of our sinfulness and should not be separated from it. "My sin is ever before me," he cries out. This awareness was healthy for David.

1. It urged him to seek cleansing.

2. It enabled him to appreciate his cleansing.

3. It demolished his pride (that had motivated him to cover his sin).

4. It cultivated a deep and real humility.

5. It urged him in the way of righteousness.
6. It gave him an aversion for returning to his sin.
7. It enabled him to accept the consequences for his sin.
8. It guided him to wise responses toward accusers (see 2 Samuel 16:10).

Those who have an aversion to looking at the sinfulness of their sexual sins and resent when others so much as mention those sins set themselves up for a superficial repentance. They want the cleansing, but they don't want the brokenness. They want other people's forgiveness (and may even demand it), but they don't want to acknowledge clearly what they are to be forgiven for.

When there is full disclosure of sin, there can be deep cleansing from sin and true forgiveness of sin. On the other hand, when full disclosure is resisted, when the sinner is more concerned about his reputation than his cleansing, we are not assured of true repentance. We cannot know that the sinner is fully intending to leave his old ways and turn his life around.

FOR FURTHER STUDY:

1. How do people avoid looking at the sinfulness of their sin?
2. Of the things you listed, which have you struggled with?
3. Is it possible to focus too much on the sinfulness of one's sin? If so, what do you think would be the results?
4. Describe the characteristics of superficial repentance.
5. Describe the results of superficial repentance.
6. Why do you think we see the sins of other people more clearly than we see our own? How should the awareness of this tendency affect how we deal with our sins? with the sins of others?

DAVID REALIZED THAT SIN HAD DAMAGED HIS HEART, AND HE SOUGHT A HEART CHANGE.

One of the most significant observations David makes in his penitential prayer is found in Verse 6. "Behold, thou desirest truth in the inward parts."

We were made in the image of God. The spiritual part of man, the "inward parts," or the heart, is the special focus of God. It is the "candle of the LORD" (Proverbs 20:27). The eye of God is continually on the heart of man, for He knows this is the control center, the place that really matters.

When we sin, we violate a sacred part of our being. We are no longer true to who we are by creation—image bearers of God. The innermost part of our being, the heart, embraces lies. Those lies become the rationale for sinful choices, sinful actions, and sinful words. We call evil good and good evil. We believe those untruths. We develop strategies to protect those untruths. We make promises by those untruths. We love, we hate, we want, we don't want, we joy, we sorrow, we fret, and we rest by lies—by the distortions that enable us to sin. And all the while, we may cover our sin with the appearance, even the declaration, that "we are true men,"[1] that we can be trusted fully.

In his repentance, David saw that by sin he had become untrue in the inmost part of his being. His heart had become untrue to God, to himself, and to those around him. He had a deceitful heart, a treacherous heart, a heart that even he could not trust—how much less God or man? David also realized that what God really wants is men and women who honestly face the treachery within. "Thou desirest truth in the inward parts!"

Looking at the same inmost being of man, God lamented through the Prophet Jeremiah, "The heart is deceitful above all things, and desperately wicked: who can know it?" (Jeremiah 17:9). The word translated "deceitful" is the same Hebrew root as the name given to Isaac's conniving son Jacob. He is literally "one who grabs the heel," one who trips from behind, one who shows a good face and covers a treacherous heart, one who turns any situation to selfish advantage.

David saw into the damage done in his heart. He recognized the Jacob within. And he cried out, "Create in me a clean heart, O God; and renew a right spirit within me" (v. 10).

Anyone who lives in immorality, and especially one who covers his sin as David did behind a cloak of righteousness, does serious damage to the inner man. True repentance not only begs for forgiveness, but it also cries out for inner renovation. A clean record is wonderful, but it does not automatically repair the damage to the soul.

The heart given over to immorality develops bad habits. Habits of reasoning. Habits of covering. Habits of manipulating situations and pressuring people to conform to its way of thinking and bend to its desires. Ways of being nice for ulterior motives. Ways of baiting people, leading them on, diverting attention, drawing attention, using facial expression and body language for advantage, laughing at the right moment, even looking indignant—all these develop into habits that are put to use in order to live out the false premises of immorality.

And the heart wrongly trained in immorality must be retrained in righteousness. Just as we have yielded our "[bodily] members as instruments of unrighteousness unto sin," so we must yield those same members "as instruments of righteousness unto God" (Romans 6:13).

The retraining must begin in the heart, but it must work

its way out through the body because the body has been a slave of sin. "Know ye not, that to whom ye yield yourselves servants to obey, his servants ye are to whom ye obey; whether of sin unto death, or of obedience unto righteousness" (Romans 6:16). The body develops unthinking (almost automatic) responses in obedience to sin, and those unthinking sinful responses must be brought to the light and be replaced with consciously chosen right responses, so that the body becomes the "servant of righteousness."

A fundamental change in the heart is accomplished through repentance. Hardened by sin, the heart must be broken in repentance. "The sacrifices of God are a broken spirit: a broken and a contrite heart, O God, thou wilt not despise" (Psalm 51:17). This produces tenderness toward God, a condition of heart that prepares the way to restore "truth in the inward parts." The heart that thrived on distorted reality must now embrace reality. Any traces of the former lies must be replaced by truth. This is an ongoing work that depends heavily on ongoing brokenness, tenderness of heart, and a penitential spirit. This is the process we wish to explore further in the next chapter.

FOR FURTHER STUDY:

1. From 2 Samuel 11, list the ways David violated his character.

2. From 2 Samuel 12:15, we would understand that David's repentance occurred after the child was born, indicating that the cover-up was extended over some time. How do you think David's secret sin affected his actions during this time?

3. Do you agree that the longer a person covers his sin,

the more damage he does to his character? Give reasons for your answer.

4. Which of the following statements, in your opinion, best describes the place of repentance in the restoration of the heart?

   a. Genuine and full repentance completely restores the heart, so that the person is actually stronger morally than before his sin.

   b. Genuine and full repentance cleanses the record, but it does nothing to restore the moral character of the heart; the repentant person is morally weaker than he was before his sin.

   c. Genuine and full repentance cleanses and fortifies the heart and prepares the heart for the rebuilding of character that needs to happen after moral failures.

DAVID'S REPENTANCE INCLUDED OPENNESS WITH THE PEOPLE INVOLVED.

This is a difficult side of repentance from sexual sin. How open shall we be? What details must be told and to whom? When parents are unfaithful, should they tell their children? If their children are too young to be told, should they be told later in life? Should this sin be announced when the offender moves to a new community? When sexual sin is private—lustful thoughts, masturbation, looking at pornography—does it need to be told to anyone else? Providing answers to these questions takes careful thought. And rather than establishing rules, the Bible seems to offer principles to guide us through these questions. These principles need to be applied wisely.

Wisdom is necessary because the guiding principles stand

somewhat in tension and call for balance. We feel the tension, for example, between openness and discretion, the tension between justice and forgiveness, the tension between compassion and standing tough, and the tension between the needs of sexual offenders and the needs of those who are hurt by the sins of offenders.

David's story involves adultery, which is only one kind of sexual sin. And though we must be careful not to run every situation through the same grid, the principles we see in David's situation can be applied to many other situations.

1. *The more public the figure, the more public the repentance needs to be.* David was a king, and his sin became known throughout the kingdom. David's psalm of penitence became part of the national songbook, and his story became part of Jewish history. It is difficult for a public figure to sin privately, and virtually impossible for him to repent privately.

2. *The level of openness should correspond to the level of relationship.* People who are affected deeply by sexual sin deserve a corresponding level of openness. When a husband is involved in masturbation and/or pornography, for example, his wife is deeply affected; and in his repentance, he must be open with her at the same level of honesty that he has hurt her. It is necessary for him to talk honestly to her about when it happened and how often and where, and it is right to discuss how he was led into sin and what can be done to ensure that he doesn't go there again. Every instance of such behavior is a sin against her directly and that sin needs to be confessed directly to her. Adultery is a sin against one's whole family, and one's whole family needs to know. If children are too young to know at the time, they will need to know later. And it is far better to learn from a penitent parent than from a mocking peer.

3. *There is freedom and healing in sharing the details with*

someone, especially someone in a responsible position. We know that only God can forgive sins. But we are admonished, "Confess your faults one to another, and pray one for another, that ye may be healed" (James 5:16). It may be a minister, a parent, a mentor, or a close friend who will be there then to stand by you, pray for you, and hold you to some measure of accountability. God told Nathan at least the basics of David's sin—adultery and murder. But David apparently disclosed the rest—how it started with observing Bathsheba bathing, how he arranged for her to come to him, the steps he took then to cover up the sin, how those steps backfired, and how he devised a plan to kill Uriah. When a person holds back details from the right people, those details can continue to produce shame in the heart. Laying bare the sin, hiding nothing from those who are responsible to know, is tremendously liberating. We receive a sense of assurance in cleansing when someone knows.

4. *There is protection in uncovering the sin to responsible people.* When Paul addressed sins of the flesh, he advised, "Let us therefore cast off the works of darkness, and let us put on the armour of light" (Romans 13:12). Sexual sins, like all sins of the flesh, easily gain a hold on us that is extremely difficult to break. Bringing those sins to the light is one way to rob them of their power. When a man confesses his sins to someone who can hold him accountable, he is preparing himself to say no the next time. He knows that what is done under cover must be brought to the light. The practice of walking in the light stands as protection against going back into the darkness. Jesus said, "Every one that doeth evil hateth the light, neither cometh to the light, lest his deeds should be reproved. But he that doeth truth cometh to the light, that his deeds may be made manifest, that they are wrought in God" (John 3:20, 21). The strong reluctance to bring sin to the light is

broken by being open with the right people.

5. *Openness sometimes results in wrong reactions and responses, but these must be accepted as part of the consequences.* As we have already noted, David's acknowledgment of sin had devastating results on his children. Both Amnon's and Absalom's sexual sins seem to have been linked in some measure to David's sexual sin (in a measure, not in full, because both sons were still responsible for their own sins). The fear that confession may negatively affect one's children or fellow church members sometimes makes people reluctant to confess their sins. The truth is that we do not determine the consequences of our sin—it certainly can and does affect others negatively. That is one reason it is so serious. But avoiding disclosure can actually increase the negative effects rather than minimize them. We must not shy away from honest, humble confession to the right people for fear of how it may affect them. Facing sin can be very embarrassing for oneself and devastating for others, but facing it is always better than hiding or minimizing it.

A related dimension here is how sins committed in singlehood affect courtship and marriage. Should such sins as masturbation, pornography, window peeping, groping, and fornication be disclosed during courtship? And if so, when? And what about experiences of being sexually abused or of sexually abusing others?

Following are some guidelines for those who have past immoral involvements and are considering a relationship:

1. *Immoral acts that involve other people should be disclosed to a prospective marriage partner.* If a young man or young woman has had sexual relations with someone and later wishes to marry someone else (or start a relationship that could lead to marriage), he/she brings an immoral record to the relationship. Even when there has been genuine repentance and

forgiveness for past sins, there should be honest acknowledgement to the prospective marriage partner. Although the sexual relationship is not synonymous with the marriage bond, nevertheless it is a bond (see 1 Corinthians 6:19). Sexual partners "know" one another in an intimate way, and it is a betrayal of trust to a prospective marriage partner not to be honest about this. Some kinds of past relationships (such as an extended sexual relationship with another partner or a relationship resulting in children) may be so entangling that marriage is not wise.

2. *When a prospective marriage partner has been sexually violated in the past or has sexually violated another person, this should be faced before marriage.* Sexual abuse is damaging. That's why it is called abuse. It leaves emotional scars and often results in spin-off problems such as difficulty in trusting, tendency to control, insecurity, over-sensitivity, and anger patterns. A person who has been sexually abused needs time to face these issues and move toward healing and maturity before marriage. When the issues surrounding sexual abuse are not resolved before marriage, they cause even more problems after marriage. Beyond that, a person who has abused other individuals needs to work through not only the relationship issues involved in the abuse, but also the underlying issues that gave rise to the abuse. An abuser is not ready for marriage, in other words, simply by apologizing to the person(s) he abused in the past.

3. *Habits of immorality need to be clearly forsaken prior to pursuing a marriage relationship.* A man or woman who has habits of masturbation, pornography, window-peeping, bestiality, etc., before marriage must not assume that marriage will resolve their sexual problems.[2] Marriage does not provide a sexual free-for-all. Restraint and self-discipline are constantly needed

to cultivate a relationship of genuine love. Sexual self-sins undermine one's ability to grow in being caring, thoughtful, wise, and sacrificial—qualities that are essential for a solid marriage relationship. Sexual sins certainly can be overcome through the grace of Jesus. But the person who does not avail himself of that grace as a single person can give no assurance that things will change after marriage.

4. *Generally, it is wise to be up front about past immoral involvements early in a relationship.* This is especially true for extensive involvements—where one has had sexual intercourse, for example, or has sexually abused others. To wait until engagement to discuss this almost invariably feels like a betrayal to the prospective partner. In the Old Testament, to wait until after marriage to disclose a compromise of virginity was considered grounds for separation, and the person guilty of sexual relations before marriage was to be stoned (see Deuteronomy 22:13, ff).

5. *When past sexual involvements need to be discussed with a prospective partner, it can be helpful to include a responsible third party.* Discussing details of sexual involvement is a sensitive venture, and that sensitivity increases when a young man and a young woman want to build a relationship. Using parents or church leaders as a third party can reduce the awkwardness of discussing this early in a relationship, and authority figures can likely be more objective in discerning what needs to be talked about and what steps may need to be taken for resolving past and present issues. There are many variables, not only in what a person has done in the past, but also in what may need to be done to resolve past issues. Seeking the counsel of older, more mature people can help keep the discussions of these matters helpful rather than unnecessarily hurtful.

Openness with the right people is an essential part of repentance, and that openness needs to be exercised initially with all parties involved (such as one's companion and those one violated in the past) as well as with all parties in the future who become involved by relationship (such as one's children and parents-in-law). This takes the grace of God and humility on our part, but we are promised God's grace when we are willing to do what is right. "But he giveth more grace. Wherefore he saith, God resisteth the proud, but giveth grace unto the humble" (James 4:6).

FOR FURTHER STUDY:

1. When a person has been guilty of sexual sins, what determines whether those sins should be confessed to the church?

2. Supposing a married male church member has had sexual relations with a single sister in the church over a period of six months. In addition, he has been involved in pornography and has sexually fondled a lady at his workplace. This man is now penitent and wishes to be restored to the church.

   a. Write out what you think would be an appropriate confession to make to the church.

   b. Suppose he has six children ranging in age from three to eighteen. What is appropriate to tell his children?

   c. Who would be appropriate people to share such details as how often, when, and where his sins took place?

   d. Would your answers to the above questions be any different if he were a pastor?

    e. Suppose this man (and his wife) would say that to tell their oldest child what he has done will result in the child leaving both home and church. What guidance would you give them?

3. What are dangers in being too general or vague in confessing one's sexual sins to the church?

4. What are dangers in being too specific or graphic in confessing one's sexual sins to the church?

5. When a young man or young woman has been involved in sexual sins as a single person and does not disclose this information until after marriage, how might this affect the marriage? How should a partner respond who hears such information?

6. List some thoughts you have for how a dating couple should handle (and should not handle) information about past sexual sins.

7. Suppose during courtship the lady learns that her prospective husband struggles regularly with masturbation. What should she do? Would your answer change if you learned that he also sometimes looks at pornography?

5

REBUILDING MORAL CHARACTER

"For this is the will of God,
even your sanctification,
that ye should abstain from fornication:
that every one of you should
know how to possess his vessel
in sanctification and honour;
not in the lust of concupiscence,
even as the Gentiles which know not God."
1 Thessalonians 4:3-5

In the last chapter, we looked at repentance, that sorrowful acknowledgement of sin and glad willingness to turn around and walk in obedience to God. Repentance is not simply saying sorry. It involves a turning from and a turning to, the forsaking of one way of life in order to begin a new way of life. Without true repentance, there is no hope of leaving our sin behind.

In this chapter, we will look at what is involved in the new

71

way of life. In Scriptural terminology, this is the way of sanctification. It is the process of being made holy, that inner transformation of the heart that restores the image of God in the sin-ruined soul.

UNDERSTANDING THE DAMAGE.

Some people mistakenly believe that confession resolves all problems with immorality. They believe the sinner needs to admit his sin, and when his sin is properly confessed and forgiven by the Father, that is that. There is no more to be done on his part. He is cleansed, and all will be well.

While God Himself clearly assures us that confession brings forgiveness, this does not mean that the forgiven person will have no more trouble with sin.

Perhaps an analogy will help. If a farmer's cows break through a fence and get into the neighbor's cornfield, they can do a lot of damage in a hurry. Suppose the farmer drives his cows back into his own field and pays for the damaged corn. That takes care of the damage, right? Does he need to do anything more? From the standpoint of the neighbor's corn, no. But we would all agree that he had better look to his fences. He had better find the weak places, the broken-down places, and he had better take the time to repair those places, or he will find himself with the same problem all over again.

When a person becomes involved in immorality, he does so by crossing the "fence" of his conscience. His lusts run against the resistance of that inner voice telling him it is wrong, and likely this conflict between desire and conscience goes on for some time before he actually sins. When he does sin, he walks through the fence, as it were. He breaks down something that has been set in his heart by God. This "breaking down" remains a broken-down area in the conscience, a breach that can offer easier access to the same sin again. The man who buys his first pornographic magazine makes an opening for himself to buy another one more easily. The longer a person has gaps in the fence of his conscience, the larger those gaps become. They get so wide that a person crosses moral boundaries almost without a thought.

Furthermore, moral sins pull us further and further into sin. The analogy of the cornfield breaks down here. When a man allows his mind to run in the way of lust, he eventually wants more. He easily moves from mental images to graphic images—that is, from lustful thoughts to pornography. And those habits eventually pull him into making advances toward women. There is no convenient stopping place.

The point here is that confession and repentance bring the wonderful forgiveness of God, and they take us back out of the forbidden territory. But they do not automatically rebuild the broken fences. Nor does a confession automatically retrain the desires. Sexual desires fed in illegitimate places will be bent on finding the weak areas again, just like the cows. The farmer who takes his cows out of the neighbor's corn may take them to his barn and give them wonderful provender. But eventually the cows will go back to the fence, and they will be drawn especially to the weak, broken-down places.

Like the farmer, a man or woman forgiven of sexual sins may feel terrible about what happened on the wrong side of the fence. But eventually the desires will return. And when they do, that man or woman had better have done something about the broken-down areas in the heart.

So, what needs to happen? There are at least three areas involved in rebuilding moral character damaged by sexual sin. One is the area of sexual desires themselves. Another is the underlying deception by which the immorality was practiced. And a third area involves the habits learned during the immorality. These three areas are not fully sequestered. They overlap considerably. But we will look at them one by one.

FOR FURTHER STUDY:

1. What is the value of accurate confession of sin?
2. Explain how some people might confess their sins to avoid the necessary work of rebuilding moral character.
3. From Psalm 51, what requests of David call for a change of heart beyond forgiveness for his sin?
4. Read Judges 16. Make a list of the character problems you see in Samson.
5. What do you think were the factors that led Samson to become like this?
6. Read 1 Kings 11:1-8. What character flaws developed in Solomon, and how did they develop?

REBUILDING MORAL CHARACTER, PART 1

THE PROBLEM OF INFLAMED SEXUAL DESIRES.

We often hear that sexual desires in themselves are not wrong. While that is true, we may fail to take into account the damage of sin. When sexual desires are satisfied in wrong ways, they do not remain as they were. Many Scriptures refer to the effects sexual sins have upon one's sexual desires.

"For this cause God gave them up unto vile affections: for even their women did change the natural use into that which is against nature: And likewise also the men, leaving the natural use of the woman, burned in their lust one toward another; men with men working that which is unseemly, and receiving in themselves that recompence of their error which was meet" (Romans 1:26, 27).

"Who being past feeling have given themselves over unto lasciviousness, to work all uncleanness with greediness" (Ephesians 4:19).

"Unto the pure all things are pure: but unto them that are defiled and unbelieving is nothing pure; but even their mind and conscience is defiled" (Titus 1:15).

"Having eyes full of adultery, and that cannot cease from sin" (2 Peter 2:14).

These Scriptures reflect various effects sexual sins have on one's sexual desires.

1. *Sexual sins can inflame the desire for the forbidden.* There is a thrill associated with the forbidden, and a man or woman who engages in sexual sins seems to be increasingly intoxicated with that thrill. The legitimate seems too mild and boring; the illegitimate gives a rush of pleasure. In reality, such a person is cutting himself off from the lasting and deeper pleasures associated with righteousness, faithfulness, and enduring marital love. He or she will never know the incredible joy of faithful love, and instead, sooner or later, will drink the dregs of the cup of sexual sins—betrayal, abandonment, separation, rejection, heartache, condemnation, and emptiness. And these may be accompanied with such sorrows as sexually transmitted diseases, broken relationships, financial ruin, a prison term, or physical violence.

When sexual pleasure comes to be associated with what is forbidden, subtle changes take place in one's sexuality. The man or woman in such a state seems driven to cross lines—not just for sex, but for the challenge of conquest, pushing the lines to find new and more daring avenues to sensuality. Ironically, the more sexual stimulation a person seeks for its sake alone, the more stimulation is needed for satisfaction. Paul describes these people as "having lost all sensitivity, they have given themselves over to sensuality so as to indulge in every kind of impurity, with a continual lust for more" (Ephesians 4:19, NIV).[1] And as we noted, the lust for the forbidden leads invariably to consequences—rejection, rage, violence, lawbreaking, abuse, and more.

2. Sexual sins can pervert sexual desires and cause what is natural to become unnatural. The more a culture gives itself to sexual pleasure, the more common sexual perversions become. Romans 1 does not teach that homosexuality is the immediate or the only result of inflamed sexual passion, but rather that uncontrolled sexual passions provide the setting in which sexual desires can be perverted. When people live for sexual pleasure, in other words, they create the dynamics for sexual perversions to develop.

This can happen in two ways. First, unbridled lust for sex can urge people to explore other avenues of sexual pleasure, with homosexuality being but one example. Second, uncontrolled sexual passions wreck homes, destroy relationships, and eliminate wholesome role models. This relational mess can do immeasurable damage to the developing identity of children, some of whom emerge as effeminate men and masculine women. Homosexuality, as we noted, is only one of the products of moral and relational confusion. And sexual sins are certainly not the only cause of confused gender identity. Who we are can be skewed even in Christian homes that practice strict moral standards. These paragraphs aren't intended to show how homosexuality develops, but to show that it is a perversion of sexuality, not a morally equal alternative.[2]

3. *Sexual sins can increase sexual desire to the point that every area of life is affected.* The lustful heart becomes increasingly enmeshed in lust. The filthy mind carries its desire for sex into the workplace, into the break room, into humor, into every conversation and every relationship and every activity of life. No place is off-limits to sexual imagination. No person is exempt from being evaluated sexually. Like radar, the desire for sexual stimulation constantly seeks to home in on potential gratification.

4. *Sexual sins can so corrupt the mind and heart that even what could be pure and good becomes tainted and defiled.* The lustful young man can turn normal interaction with a young woman into visual gratification (even in church meetings). A married man can use his wife to feed his lustful desires. Lust can so pervade a man's heart that a pure woman finds it uncomfortable even to be in his presence, though he may not be touching her physically.

5. *Sexual sins can so inflame sexual desires that they push aside all moral restraint and control the mind and will, and thus the body.* Sexual sins are addicting. They pull the mind back and turn the feet repeatedly toward the paths of sin. When the eyes are "full of adultery," that is all they can see in the opposite sex. As the Bible puts it, the sexual sinner "cannot cease from sin" (2 Peter 2:14). His moral strength is ruined, and his desires pull him back over and over, even after he comes to hate his sin.

So when we say that sexual desires are right in themselves, let us be very careful what we mean. They are right in the God-given sense. But they are *not* right in their sin-inflamed forms. These are gross mutations.

FOR FURTHER STUDY:

1. What expressions in Romans 1 indicate clearly that sexual desires can become wrong desires?
2. When a person feeds the desire for the forbidden, what legitimate joys does he ruin?
3. Describe as accurately as you can how legitimate joys surpass the thrill of the forbidden in the area of our sexuality.
4. Think of someone you know (or from the Bible) who indulged in forbidden sexual pleasures, and list the negative results that came with those thrills.
5. In your own words, list two ways people move into homosexuality in a culture where sexual passions are given free rein.
6. What wording in Romans 1 indicates that homosexuality is abnormal—that it is a perversion of sexual desires?
7. List some of the things that are damaged in a person obsessed with sexual thoughts and desires.
8. What are some practical things a lady can do when she is in the presence of a sexually obsessed man?
9. What are some practical things a man can do when he must relate to a sexually obsessed woman?

DEALING WITH INFLAMED SEXUAL PASSIONS.

So, how does a person deal with sexual desires that have become controlling monsters in his life? Romans 6 is very helpful here. The "body of sin" can indeed be dealt with. The means are ruthless, but the effect is life-changing.

"Knowing this, that our old man is crucified with him, that the body of sin might be destroyed, that henceforth we should not serve sin. Likewise reckon ye also yourselves to be dead indeed unto sin, but alive unto God through Jesus Christ our Lord. Let not sin therefore reign in your mortal body, that ye should obey it in the lusts thereof" (Romans 6:6, 11, 12).

The power of sexual desires can be broken through death and resurrection with Christ. What really does this mean?

In Romans 6 we have what some have termed the "identification doctrines." Paul says we have been "crucified with Christ," we have been "buried with him," and we have been "raised with him." And in the context, he clearly and repeatedly states this as the means by which the power of sin is broken in our lives.

"How shall we, that are dead to sin, live any longer therein?" (v. 2).

"Our old man is crucified with him, that the body of sin might be destroyed, that henceforth we should not serve sin" (v. 6).

"He that is dead is freed from sin" (v. 7).

"Likewise reckon ye also yourselves to be dead indeed unto sin" (v. 11).

"Let not sin therefore reign in your mortal body, that ye should obey it in the lusts thereof" (v. 12).

"For sin shall not have dominion over you" (v. 14).

"Being then made free from sin, ye became the servants of righteousness" (v. 18).

"But now being made free from sin" (v. 22).

Without question, Paul is saying that in our dying with Christ, something happens that delivers us from the power of sin. People whose inflamed sexual desires have become merciless tyrants need this deliverance. How does it happen? How do we die with Christ? How are we buried with Him? And how are we resurrected with Him? Is this only a lofty idea? What is the practical reality for us?

This passage emphasizes two factors that affect the believer's spiritual union with Jesus: 1) Knowing. 2) Reckoning.

But before we discuss these, we must look briefly at the real culprit. Paul speaks of "sin" in this passage in a sense that is more fundamental than an action. He is not dealing with the sin of lying, the sin of adultery, or the sin of stealing. He is dealing with sin—the entity of sin, the indwelling moral twistedness in all of us. Some refer to this as the "nature of sin." Paul simply calls it sin. When he says that "henceforth we should not serve sin" (v. 6) or when he says, "Let not sin therefore reign in your mortal body" (v. 12), he is not referring to a particular sin we do, but to the sinfulness within us that produces all the particular sins, including sexual sins.

There will be no victory over sins until we deal with sin. To be free of sexual sins, we must lay our ax to that root of sin, the granddaddy within.

THE IMPORTANCE OF KNOWING.

Deliverance from sin involves knowing. "**Know** ye not, that so many of us as were baptized into Jesus Christ were baptized into his death?" (v. 3). "**Knowing** this, that our old man is crucified with him, that the body of sin might be destroyed, that henceforth we should not serve sin" (v. 6). "**Knowing** that Christ being raised from the dead dieth no more; death hath no more dominion over him" (v. 9).

Gaining victory over sin involves a knowing; that is, it involves acquainting the heart and mind with truth. This starts with objective realities. Simply, we must embrace the disturbing reality that we are sinners. We must know that our sins carry the sentence of eternal damnation. We must know that in ourselves we are hopelessly lost. We will never make progress against sin until we face honestly the hopelessness of our condition, until we truly give up the delusion that we are not so bad. We must know our sinfulness.

But that is not all we must know. Sinners bound by sexual sins can know the truth about themselves without being delivered. We must know Jesus and what He has done for us. We must know that He left glory and came to earth as a man. We must know that He died. We must know that He died for our sins. We must know that in His death for our sins, He was fully innocent, and we were fully guilty. And we must know that when He died, we were spiritually WITH Him. Our sin nails us to His cross, uniting us to Him in His death. We must know Jesus, of course, not simply in a factual way or in the historical context of His earthly life. We must know Him in spiritual acquaintance as a living person.

The knowledge of our sinfulness coupled with the knowledge of our Saviour is crushing truth. Knowing what He did for us as a result of our sin is overwhelming. We are broken. The longer we look at the Saviour hanging on the cross for our sins, the deeper the spear goes into our own soul. By our sin, we are nailed to the cross with Him. We must embrace this truth in our hearts, painful and humbling though it is, because it is in our union with Jesus in His death that we experience the crucifixion of *sin* within us—that indwelling bent, that nature to go our own way. How can we sin, knowing what we know about our sin and our Saviour, knowing how integrally we were joined to Him in His death!

If a mother just witnessed her young son being run over by a truck, how could she sit down and enjoy a meal? And suppose the mother had accidentally pushed her son in front of the truck, causing him to die. His death would be inseparable from her act. And the horrible death she had witnessed, plus the brutal knowledge that she had caused it, would "kill" her appetite. All desire for food would be gone. Even so, when the knowledge of what Jesus did for us and what we did to Him is fully flooding our hearts and minds, the appetite for sin dies.

THE IMPORTANCE OF RECKONING.

The second emphasis in Romans 6 in dealing with sin is that we must "reckon" ourselves dead to sin, or in more familiar terms, we are to count it so. "Likewise **reckon** ye also yourselves to be dead indeed unto sin, but alive unto God through Jesus Christ our Lord" (v. 11).

We are to count ourselves as dead to sin. That is, we must cultivate thinking that we no longer practice sin, we no longer listen to its voice, we no longer pay it any attention. Our acquaintance with Jesus shows us what sin really is, and we count ourselves dead to the pull of sin, dead to sin's desires.

This is only one side of the experience, of course. We are dead to sin in order to be alive to God. We have seen what God has done to redeem us from sin. We have seen the sacrifice of His Son. We have seen God's love. We are growing in acquaintance and relationship with Jesus, and He has become our new master. We are alive to His voice, alive to His purposes for our lives, alive to pleasing Him.

Being dead to sin is nothing apart from being alive to God. We are not only nailed to the cross with Jesus, but we are raised with Him. The old way of living—doing what *sin* says—is dead. That life is the "old man," or the former way of life. The new way of living—doing what *Jesus* says—is the "new man," the way of life we now pursue.

Being dead to sin and alive to God, of course, is a matter

of faith. It is a spiritual experience, a work of grace that happens within us. We count it so by faith. In our hearts we have settled the matter—we have died with Jesus, and we have been raised to life with Him. We can testify with the Apostle Paul, "I am crucified [literally "have been crucified"] with Christ: nevertheless I live; yet not I, but Christ liveth in me: and the life which I now live in the flesh I live by the faith of the Son of God, who loved me, and gave himself for me" (Galatians 2:20).

There can be no victory over sin, no rebuilding of moral character, without a spiritual union with Jesus in His death and resurrection. We render the nature of sin powerless through Christ and through Him alone. Jesus is not only our Saviour in the sense of forgiving our past sins, but He must also be our Saviour in the sense of presently, day-by-day saving us from sin. Any man or woman who wishes to be free from the bondage of sexual sins must cling heart and soul to Jesus. He is the true Saviour, and He is big enough to break any chain, free any captive.

FOR FURTHER STUDY:

1. What might be some practical ways to guide the mind in "knowing" one's sinfulness? What would be some ways to acquaint our hearts with the Saviour?

2. What is the result of knowing our sinfulness without knowing the Saviour?

3. Describe in your own words what the following expressions mean for you:
    a. "I was crucified with Christ."
    b. "I was buried with Christ."
    c. "I was raised from the dead with Christ."

    d. "I am seated with Christ." (See Ephesians 2:6.)

4. As honestly as you can, tell how well you have done in reckoning yourself dead to sin and alive to God.

5. What are some differences between an earthly relationship and our relationship with God?

6. Suppose one day you don't "feel" alive to God. What are healthy responses to such feelings? What would be unhealthy responses? How can believers live above their feelings (sometimes act contrary to them) without devaluing or totally ignoring them?

7. What are the results of reckoning ourselves dead to sin but neglecting to reckon ourselves alive to God? What might be the results of reckoning ourselves alive to God and neglecting to reckon ourselves dead to sin?

REBUILDING MORAL CHARACTER, PART 2

THE PROBLEM OF DECEPTION.

All sin is based on deception. If we could see sin as it really is, if we could always see where it leads and what it does, we would run from it in horror. Sexual sins in particular are surrounded with attractive covers. There is probably no area where Satan has gotten away with making poison and filth look so desirable as in the area of sexual sins. Unmasked, sexual sin is utterly stupid.[3]

One problem with yielding to sexual sins is that we take the deceptions into our heart and mind. We not only think wrong thoughts, but we think they are right. The wrong ideas are so imbedded we hardly realize they are there. Furthermore, sometimes we can know sexual sin is wrong, but we still believe the deceptions that make it attractive. In other words, we can label adultery sin, but still view it as more attractive than faithfulness in marriage. We may stop short of doing the sin, but we stop regretfully—thinking life really would be more enjoyable if we could live without restraints on our sexual desires. That is plain stupid, but we have a hard time seeing it so.

To rebuild moral character, we must unmask the deceptions of sexual sin. We must tear out the twisted frameworks by which sin is made to look attractive and replace them with the straight and true principles found in God's Word.

Let's list some of the deceptive ideas that form the rationale for sexual sin:

1. The forbidden is better than the permissible (i.e., adultery is more enjoyable than faithfulness, or pornography is better than seeing people properly dressed).
2. Whatever doesn't hurt anyone is okay.
3. Whatever doesn't involve anyone else is okay.
4. I can do it as long as no one knows.
5. When the opposite sex is provocative, I am not responsible for my lustful thoughts and actions.
6. Sex is more important than relationship.
7. A person without a companion has to do *something* to satisfy sexual desires.
8. Marriage gives a person the right to have sex according to desire.
9. A companion should cooperate with anything I enjoy.
10. When a companion doesn't cooperate sexually, I am justified in pressuring him/her to meet my desires.
11. A companion who doesn't cooperate sexually is being selfish.
12. When a companion doesn't cooperate sexually, I have to get it somewhere else.

The list of deceptions and their variations is endless. When we want to rebuild moral character, we must identify the deceptions we have embraced or found attractive. This takes honesty and perseverance. Unfortunately, lovers of sin become lovers of lies. And rooting out the lies can be hard work because we have a hard time being honest about the reasoning of sin. We have a hard time acknowledging that we actually operate by such warped ideas.

When we have identified the lies imbedded in our thoughts and motives, we can expose our minds to truth. This involves truth about lust as well as truth about moral purity. The Bible has many passages to help us in this, including stories as well as direct teaching. The stories of David and Bathsheba, Samson and his women, the Levite and his concubine, Hosea and Gomer, and the unfaithful wife in Proverbs 7—these all provide living examples to show us the truth about lust. Many other passages teach the truth directly.

"Lust not after her beauty in thine heart; neither let her take thee with her eyelids. For by means of a whorish woman a man is brought to a piece of bread: and the adulteress will hunt for the precious life" (Proverbs 6:25, 26).

"But whoso committeth adultery with a woman lacketh understanding: he that doeth it destroyeth his own soul. A wound and dishonour shall he get; and his reproach shall not be wiped away" (Proverbs 6:32, 33).

"Ye have heard that it was said by them of old time, Thou shalt not commit adultery: But I say unto you, That whosoever looketh on a woman to lust after her hath committed adultery with her already in his heart" (Matthew 5:27, 28).

"For this is the will of God, even your sanctification, that ye should abstain from fornication: that every one of you should know how to possess his vessel in sanctification and honour; not in the lust of concupiscence, even as the Gentiles which know not God: that no man go beyond and defraud his brother in any matter: because that the Lord is the avenger of all such, as we also have forewarned you and testified. For God hath not called us unto uncleanness, but unto holiness" (1 Thessalonians 4:3-7).

From these verses, we can unmask deceptions surrounding immorality. The truths about lust and immorality are hard and they are many.

IMMORAL THOUGHTS AND ACTIONS

1. Stir desires that can never be satisfied.
2. Lead to misery and guilt.
3. Ruin relationships.
4. Corrupt our sexual capacities, causing them to become inordinate or perverted.
5. Undermine manliness and moral strength.
6. Make feminine beauty artificial and cheap.
7. Lead to weakness and bondage.
8. Set in motion consequences that follow a person for years, even after forgiveness and cleansing have taken place.
9. Stir jealousies, rivalries, and bitter conflict.
10. Carry intense shame.
11. Feed selfishness.
12. Destroy integrity and the ability to trust.

When we follow the deceitfulness of sexual sin, we simply do not realize the price we will pay. That deceitfulness needs to be unmasked if we are to be delivered. The rebuilding of moral character involves an "opening of the eyes," a new ability to see things as they really are. We cultivate this ability by regularly looking into the Word of God for insight. In that light, we begin more and more to see the deceitfulness of sin.

But the truth about immorality is only one side. The Bible has much to say about the beauty and value of moral purity. Consider these truths:

1. Moral purity is in harmony with our creation and with our Creator.
2. Morally pure relationships are solid and satisfying.
3. It is manly to respect the purity of women, to control sexual drives, and to avoid sources of temptation.
4. It is a mark of true feminine beauty to be pure, to cultivate character, and to be discreet in word, manner, and appearance.
5. Moral purity brings glory to God.
6. All Heaven's resources stand behind those who choose to be morally pure.
7. Moral purity produces greater enjoyment and fulfillment than immoral actions ever can.
8. Moral purity is to be admired.
9. Moral purity gives the freedom to look at people without shame.
10. Moral purity provides a setting for true manhood and womanhood to develop.
11. Moral purity strengthens relationships.
12. Moral purity leaves a rich legacy that can enhance the strength and character of future generations.

We simply cannot place a price tag on the value of a morally pure life or the fulfillment that such a life brings. When we honor the truth about moral purity, men can be real men, and women can be real women.

To rebuild moral character, we must not only identify the deceptions by which we have lived, but we must replace those deceptions with truth. This comes about as we immerse our minds repeatedly in the truth. It is helpful to read and study the stories in the Bible. It does us good to contemplate the misery of men like David and Samson when they violated moral standards. And we can learn much from people like Rahab and others who were redeemed from lives of sin and shame. Incidentally, Boaz, a man of high moral standards, was the son of Rahab. From Rahab and Boaz, we are encouraged that corrupted lives can be redeemed. Moral character can indeed be rebuilt. And when that takes place, the sins of one generation do not need to be repeated by the next.

We should note here a particular deception that often accompanies sexual relations, a deception tied directly to the nature of sexual union. The sexual union forms a bond that carries a strong sense of obligation. Ironically, a man who has had sexual relations with a woman other than his wife may hold his sense of obligation to her above his marriage covenant. Within this illicit bond he may feel compelled to fulfill promises he made to her even though they violate the lifelong covenant he made with his wife. He will even describe this as a matter of honor. "I promised, and I can't go back on my word." In his mind, he has to provide a place for her to live, give her a vehicle to use, provide for her child, or not abandon her, even though all of this stabs the heart and soul of his own wife. In light of the violation to his wife, such "honor" is utterly stupid, of course. He needs to see those obligations for what they are—violations of his honor—and repent of them. But while the new union is fresh in his mind, he has a hard time freeing himself from the deceptive sense of obligation.

An unfaithful woman (or an empty single lady) can be

caught in a similar sense of obligation, not to provide for a man's material needs but to meet a relational need. A woman may be snared into a sexual relationship with a man due to her compassion for his loneliness or rejection. And she will be loath to break off the relationship if she fears that the man will "not make it" without her love. In her twisted thinking, he needs her, and she finds it extremely difficult to leave him without any hope. She fears he will go into depression, that he will commit suicide, or that he will "do something terrible" if she leaves him. And she often is convinced no one understands him like she does.

FOR FURTHER STUDY:

1. From the list of deceptions, identify the ones you have struggled with. Then arrange your list in order, starting with what is the most dangerous or the greatest problem for you.

2. What Scripture verses speak to these deceptions? (You may choose verses not listed in the text.) Write out specifically how the verses address the deceptions.

3. Which of these verses would be most helpful for you to meditate on to keep you from sexual sins?

4. Consider the list of truths about immoral thoughts and actions. Choose one that is especially important to you and tell why it is so. What truths about immorality might you add from your own experience?

5. Consider the list of truths about moral purity. What truths might you add from your own experience?

Rebuilding Moral Character, Part 3

THE PROBLEM OF BAD HABITS.

We have seen that rebuilding moral character calls for a death and resurrection with Christ and requires a renewing of our minds—a shift from thinking falsehoods to thinking truth. These changes are foundational to dealing with bad habits, and yet we need to give consideration to habits themselves.

Simply speaking, habits are learned behaviors. Actually, it is fortunate for us that we can do things by habit—when we walk we don't need to decide whether to place the left foot forward or the right foot, to adjust for a change of surface, or to avoid an object in our path. We do these things unconsciously, especially in familiar territory such as our own house. Our mind may be occupied with thinking about a relative's health or calculating how to divide this week's paycheck while we walk a winding path around furniture, toys, children, and laundry.

This is the blessing of habits.

But the blessing is a curse when it comes to sin. Just as the body learns to do beneficial things without thinking, so it learns to sin without thinking, so to speak. When we have trained the body to follow sexual impulses, we learn to shift the eyes to assess the bodies, clothing, words, and body language of the opposite sex. We learn to do this with little conscious thought that we are doing it. We learn to modulate the voice, move the eyes, shift hips and shoulders, laugh and react in ways that correspond to sexual desires that drive us. Such behaviors as flirting, lusting, and off-color humor can be trained into our bodies so that we may not think of what we are doing. At a deeper level, we may habitually twist the meaning of words and events to be suggestive, or we may justify and excuse our immoral actions, or we may cover up our suggestive words or actions—that is, we may be doing all these things by habit, with little conscious thought. Whatever we *do* without conscious thought, however, will never be *changed* without conscious thought. We can "not think" to do something, but we can't "not think" to quit doing it.

Bad habits need to be addressed in the process of rebuilding moral character. What has been trained in must be trained out. The eyes that learned to look must be trained to avoid looking. The mind that was trained to cover and justify must be trained to expose and confess. The body that was trained to sin must be trained to do right. Paul addresses this clearly and repeatedly in Romans 6.

"Neither **yield** ye your members as instruments of unrighteousness unto sin: but **yield** yourselves unto God, as those that are alive from the dead, and your members as instruments of righteousness unto God" (v. 13). "Know ye not, that to whom ye **yield** yourselves servants to obey, his servants ye are to whom ye obey; whether of sin unto death, or of obedience unto righteousness?" (v. 16). "For as ye have **yielded** your members servants to uncleanness and to iniquity unto iniquity; even so now **yield** your members servants to righteousness unto holiness" (v. 19).

The body members that were yielded to sin must be consciously yielded to God. Job said, "I made a covenant with mine eyes; why then should I think upon a maid?" (Job 31:1). To Timothy, Paul wrote, "I will therefore that men pray every where, lifting up holy hands, without wrath and doubting" (1 Timothy 2:8). Zacharias prophesied that part of the ministry of his son, John, would be "to guide our feet into the way of peace" (Luke 1:79). To the Romans, Paul wrote, "I beseech you therefore, brethren, by the mercies of God, that ye present your bodies a living sacrifice, holy, acceptable unto God, which is your reasonable service" (Romans 12:1). The Greek word translated here as "present" is the same as the word translated "yield" in Romans 6.

All of these verses demonstrate the "yielding" of our bodies to the righteous intentions of God. That is, we are to consciously give our bodies and the members of our bodies over to the service of God—to do His will. We are to train new ways of seeing, talking, laughing, and conducting ourselves into the members of our body. Even our body language is to reflect the new goals, new thinking, and new choices of the renewed heart.

FOR FURTHER STUDY:

1. List some good habits you have.
2. Name a habit you have tried to break (other than a habit of sexual sin). Describe what difficulties you have faced in breaking the habit.
3. Name the habits involving sexual thoughts or actions that you have struggled with. Be as thorough as you can.
4. For each habit you named, tell what you have done to break this habit and describe the results.
5. For each habit you named, tell what body members need to be yielded to God. Then take this before the Lord and ask Him what would be a meaningful way for you to yield your members to Him. This could be a special "presenting" of your body to the Lord, or it could be a written covenant, or it could be a combination of

both. It could be private between you and the Lord, or it could include a trusted friend.

ENGAGING THE HEART.

The formal yielding of the body to God is helpful only as the heart's actual intent is to do so. In other words, it accompanies spiritual union with Christ and transformation of the mind; it does not replace those experiences. The retrained body is the servant of the renewed mind. When it is so, yielding the body to God is a very positive experience. Rebuilding character is not simply learning to say no to sin, but learning to say yes to God. Even more, it is training the body in the ways of righteousness so that even as it was "automatically" inclined to sin, it becomes "automatically" inclined to righteousness. The habits that enabled us to sin almost without thinking are replaced with habits that enable us to do right almost without thinking.

This training starts, however, with great effort, just as any worthwhile training. We did not learn to walk, ride bike, or whistle without concentration, effort, repeated effort, and much practice. But the effort pays off, so that eventually we can do these things almost on "autopilot," with little conscious thought.

Retraining can be even harder than training, however, because we have to make conscious effort to avoid falling back into old habits. In years past, for example, a person who switched from driving a horse and buggy to driving an automobile had not only to learn how to do something new, but he had to quit doing it the old way. Speaking to the car or pulling on the steering wheel did not bring the same results as speaking to the horse or pulling on the reins.

ENLISTING GOD'S HELP.

The person who wishes to change from yielding his body to sin to yielding it to God will find that conscious effort is necessary. The new ways may feel awkward at first. Slipping back may seem so natural. But fortunately, for training the body in the ways of righteousness, we have divine help. By yielding to God, we invite the presence of the Holy Spirit, that mighty One given to us to keep the flesh in subjection. "Walk in the Spirit," Paul writes, "and ye shall not fulfil the lust of the flesh. For the flesh lusteth against the Spirit, and the Spirit against the flesh" (Galatians 5:16, 17). Praise God for the indwelling Spirit who takes the flesh as His special assignment!

So even as we put forth conscious and diligent effort to retrain our tongue, our eyes, our hands, and our feet in the ways of God, we do so with a prayer on our lips. We struggle with all our might even while we rely on the strength and grace of the Spirit within us to change from the old ways to the new ways. The Apostle Paul put it this way: "Work out your own salvation with fear and trembling. For it is God which worketh in you both to will and to do of his good pleasure" (Philippians 2:12, 13). Our efforts are necessary but they are not enough. We work hard, and at the same time, we look to the Lord for divine assistance.

A proper balance here is vitally important, for people fall into error on either side. On the one hand, a man or woman who has fallen into patterns of immorality will try hard, and try repeatedly, to be free of the bondage, only to fail over and over and never really be free. This person knows the importance of giving personal effort, but he may not understand how to avail himself of divine grace. Or he may understand but be unwilling to really leave his sin. The most common hindrance to availing oneself of grace is failing to meet the condition of humility. God gives grace to the humble (see James 4:6), to those whose hearts are broken, to those who are fully willing to come under the hand of God, to those who are done with self-government. A lack of humility and brokenness leaves people where they never find divine grace, and it results in fruitless efforts—trying over and over to quit sexual sin in their own strength and never making it.

On the other side of the issue are those who place all of the responsibility on the Lord. They know they do not have what it takes to conquer sexual sin, and so they say God must do it for them. They no longer try. They say they have prayed to the Lord to free them from this problem, and now they will wait on Him to do it. Those living on this side of the problem range from the religious to the profane. Some speak in holy language of the sovereignty of God, and say He does whatever He pleases and He can change them any time He sets His mind to do so. Others speak accusingly of God—He gave them these sexual drives and He is responsible to change them if He wants them changed. In any case, those who see only the need of divine help neglect to take personal responsibility (or use "grace" as a way of avoiding it). They are unwilling to make the choices and put forth the effort God requires for leaving their sin.

The Scriptural balance is that we work at change—and we work hard—and all the while we work, we confess that we don't have what it takes in ourselves. We rely on the Lord to work in us that which we cannot do.

SUMMARY

We have seen that rebuilding moral character wrecked by sexual sin involves at least three things: 1) Dealing with the twisted desires. 2) Identifying deceptions and replacing them with truth. 3) Retraining the body from following habits of sin to following habits of righteousness.

Sexual desires inflamed by sin become controlling monsters that, along with all the rest of the self-life, must die with Christ and be raised to new life with Him. In "newness of life," then, the mind must be renewed, tearing down the old way of thinking and rebuilding a whole new mindset based on truth. Habits formed in sin must be consciously rejected, and the body, dedicated now to the service of Jesus, must be retrained to speak and act out of the new heart. This is the rebuilding of moral character. It does not happen by chance. It does not happen automatically with confession and repentance (nor does it happen without them). It is a process. It happens by living a new kind of life on purpose. It happens by living in union with Jesus.

FOR FURTHER STUDY:

1. In your own words, write out what is God's will for you concerning your sexuality. Include both what He does not want (for you specifically) and what He does want.

2. Looking at what you wrote, try to describe what your part is. That is, what do you need to do in order to live out God's will for you?

3. Looking at what you need to do, where do you feel particularly needy? Write out a prayer acknowledging your need to God and asking for His divine grace. What might you do to keep this prayer in your heart and on your lips?

4. Read 1 John 5:14, 15. How do these verses relate to your prayer?

5. In your own struggle against sexual sins, do you think you have relied too much on your own strength or expected God to do your part? Have you struggled with blaming God for not doing what He expects you to do? Are there things you could do to keep both your responsibility and your dependence on God in healthy balance?

6. Considering the three sections in this chapter, which is most significant for you, considering where you are in building moral character? Explain your answer.

6

WORKING THROUGH
CONSEQUENCES

"And David said unto Nathan,
I have sinned against the LORD.
And Nathan said unto David,
The LORD also hath put away thy sin;
thou shalt not die.
Howbeit, because by this deed
thou hast given great occasion
to the enemies of the LORD to blaspheme,
the child also that is born
unto thee shall surely die."
2 Samuel 12:13, 14

David's repentance for his sin was genuine, and so was God's forgiveness. But forgiveness does not take away all the consequences for sin. In the weeks and months that follow sexual sin (or its disclosure), come a multitude of difficulties that stem directly from it. These difficulties can include legal charges, church discipline, and family and marital conflicts.

For example, even when the offender is penitent and cooperative, the spouse and children of an unfaithful companion typically go through a series of struggles in attempting to understand what happened, forgive the offender, and rebuild trust.

For a man or woman ensnared in sexual sin, how he or she responds to consequences is extremely important. It can make the difference between living in victory or falling back into sin. How one responds to consequences can also have a large bearing on how long and how powerfully those consequences affect one's life and relationships. The nature of our responses can either increase the effects of those consequences or decrease them.

So the person who has repented of immorality needs to learn to respond wisely and humbly to people and situations in the months and years following repentance. Although the sins can be forgiven instantaneously, the effects cannot be erased from the lives of those involved.

Let's look at several points about the consequences of sexual sins and then at how to respond properly to those consequences.

CONSEQUENCES ARE INEVITABLE.

This is a hard truth. All sins have consequences. And yet, not all sins have equal consequences. Furthermore, some sins affect us personally, and some affect our relationships. Since our sexuality was specifically designed for our interpersonal needs, many consequences for sexual sins are interpersonal. And since our sexuality is a fundamental part of who we are, sexual sins have serious consequences. These consequences are many, and they are inevitable.

A person may think some sexual sins are private. Such sins

as lustful thoughts, pornography, and masturbation can be done alone, with no one seeing or knowing what we have done. And yet, although a person may sin in private, he can rarely keep the consequences to himself. We are "free" to sin, in one sense, but if we sin, we are not in control of what that sin may do to us or to those we love. It is a lesson learned too late by many.

When David spent that hour with Bathsheba, he had no idea how high the cost would be for himself and for his family. Let's have a look at what resulted from David's sin of adultery. Consider especially the interpersonal implications of each of these consequences.

- Bathsheba became pregnant.
- David tried to attach the responsibility to Uriah, only to have it backfire.
- David became desperate and arranged to kill Uriah.
- God showed Nathan, David's trusted prophet, what David had done, and Nathan had to confront David.
- Bathsheba's child died.
- The whole nation learned about David's sin.
- Unbelievers learned about David's sin, and it became a disgrace to David's God.
- David's oldest son Amnon lusted after Tamar and arranged to rape her.
- Amnon then disgraced Tamar by driving her away, setting up murderous attitudes between David's children.
- Absalom (full brother to Tamar) eventually killed Amnon, resulting in alienation between David and Absalom.
- Absalom reacted to the alienation by becoming bitter toward David and took over the throne, causing David to run for his life.
- While David was escaping, probably at one of the lowest

points in his life, Shimei threw dirt and insults at him.

- Back in Jerusalem, Absalom committed adultery with some of David's servant wives, openly insulting David.
- A battle followed in which 20,000 Israelites were killed, many of whom had been part of Absalom's treacherous conspiracy.
- David's son Absalom was killed.
- David's trusted advisor, Ahithophel (grandfather of Bathsheba), sided with Absalom; and when his own counsel was ignored, he committed suicide.
- David's sons postured for the throne—after David's death, Solomon killed Adonijah for his aspirations.

How true was the word of the Lord—"The sword shall never depart from thine house" (2 Samuel 12:10)! David paid and paid and paid for his sin.

Not everyone experiences the exact consequences David did, but consequences always follow immorality. The writer of Proverbs put it this way: "Can a man take fire in his bosom, and his clothes not be burned? Can one go upon hot coals, and his feet not be burned? So he that goeth in to his neighbour's wife; whosoever toucheth her shall not be innocent" (6:27-29). Or as the NIV says, "No one who touches her will go unpunished."

When sexual desires are satisfied within the bounds of marriage as directed by God, they are like a well-tended furnace that warms the home. But disregarding God's boundaries for sex is like taking burning embers out of the furnace. Someone is going to be burned, and the whole house may go up in flames. As we have said before, the consequences for sexual sins are inevitable, and they are serious. Only a fool thinks he can get by.

CONSEQUENCES CAN BE BOTH PREVENTIVE AND REDEMPTIVE.

Many a person has kept himself from sexual sin because he knew there would be consequences. The sin may look attractive, and the person may be sorely tempted to yield, but he thinks of what will happen. The name of God will be disgraced. A companion will be betrayed. Children will be disappointed and likely embittered. The community will talk. It may mean a loss of position. Certainly it will result in a loss of reputation.

Randy Alcorn records that a church elder once confessed to him that at times he had had serious temptations to commit adultery. "I'd like to say that my love for God and for my wife were enough to keep me from falling," the man said. "But it came down to *sheer terror*. I was certain that if I traveled that road, God would let my life turn miserable." Commenting on this, Alcorn says, "The fear of God shouldn't scare us out of our wits; it should scare us *into* them. 'The fear of the LORD is a fountain of life, turning a man from the snares of death' (Proverbs 14:27)."[1]

In Proverbs 7 we read about a "simple" young man who was led into sexual sin by a seductive woman. This uninformed man did not understand the consequences. He may have known it was wrong to have sexual relations with a married woman, but, as the writer says, "He goeth after her straightway, as an ox goeth to the slaughter, or as a fool to the correction of the stocks; till a dart strike through his liver; as a bird hasteth to the snare, and knoweth not that it is for his life" (Proverbs 7:22, 23). Not knowing the consequences, he is vulnerable to the attraction of the sin.

This tells us that one way to avoid sexual sin is to look honestly and soberly at the consequences. Studying the lives of

David, Samson, and others who indulged in sexual sin can strengthen our resolve not to sin. And we might add here that stories (or songs) that portray sexual sin without any consequences are dangerous. Romance novels, soap operas, and country music create the illusion that sexual sin is exhilarating and satisfying, that forbidden relationships are sometimes the best, and that sexual sins do not destroy us but are a means to fulfillment.

Knowing the truth about the consequences of sexual sins can be a preventive against sin. This is part of the wisdom often discussed in the Proverbs. And such wisdom serves "to deliver thee from the strange woman, even from the stranger which flattereth with her words; which forsaketh the guide of her youth, and forgetteth the covenant of her God. For her house inclineth unto death, and her paths unto the dead" (Proverbs 2:16-18).

Consequences for sexual sins can also be redemptive. That is, they can serve to draw the sinner back to the right way and to keep him committed to the right way. Consequences for sexual sin often strike viciously. "For jealousy is the rage of a man: therefore he will not spare in the day of vengeance" (Proverbs 6:34).

Owen, for example, was a married man who sexually fondled several adolescent girls in town one day. When the girls' fathers learned what Owen had done, they came out to his house with baseball bats. They were so angry that they were not willing to wait on due process of the law to deal with Owen. Fortunately for Owen, they did not find him. But he did have to face legal consequences for his sin, including being placed in a center to receive help.

For years Owen had hidden his sexual sins under a cloak of externally strict zeal in the church. Unmasking the true contents of his heart was a bitterly fought process, but eventually, Owen opened his heart to God in brokenness. He tearfully confessed his sins to God and then to his wife and children. The serious consequences had served to strip the covers from his sin and then to bring him to the throne of God begging for forgiveness.

Owen's case shows that the hold of sexual sins can be so binding and the drugging effect can be so blinding that it may take a lightning-bolt type of trouble to bring the sinner to reality.

The consequences for sexual sins, however, are not all immediate upon repentance. Some of the more difficult effects of sexual sins are those that come years later. When a sinner is penitent and receives the forgiveness of God, this often results in forgiveness from family and church members as well, at least among Christians. In a forgiving atmosphere, a repentant sinner may assume he can now put this sin behind him and go on with a clean slate.

In one way he can. He is forgiven. But he will still face consequences. As David's life shows, he may face multiplied sorrows in the years ahead. Younger ones who followed him and looked up to him, may turn to the same sin and then blame him for it. Somewhere along the way, there will usually be a Shimei who throws dirt, seemingly at the most inopportune time. These ongoing consequences of sexual sins will often seem unfair. People may misread motives. Rumors may spread. Assumptions may be made. Lines may be drawn. Charges may be leveled—all in ways that seem very unfair to the repentant sinner.

The most common temptation in the months and years following repentance from sexual sin is the temptation to become resentful and bitter. At times a repentant person may feel people are not forgiving, that they are refusing to trust, and that it is not worth trying to do right. Some people who respond in brokenness to the "lightning bolt" consequences eventually fall back into sin when "Shimei" begins throwing dirt. Some sexual offenders use the unfairness of their experiences to justify their return to immorality.

The consequences that result in resentment and bitterness for some people, however, are actually redemptive for others. God can use "unfair" situations to bring us back to the right way, to keep our hearts tender, to cultivate the sense of unworthiness in forgiveness, and to keep us on the path of righteousness. Whether these consequences serve to help us or to destroy us will be determined by our responses. So after the following questions, we will consider some wrong responses to consequences for sexual sins, as well as how God wants us to respond.

FOR FURTHER STUDY:

1. In this chapter, we have explored consequences David experienced for his sexual sin. Consider one of the following Bible characters, and make a list of the consequences he or she experienced: a. Samson (Judges 14-16), b. Judah (Genesis 38), c. Dinah (Genesis 34)

2. In Genesis 39, we read that Joseph was faithful in a time of sexual temptation. What consequences did Joseph suffer for being faithful?

3. Try to project what might have happened had Joseph yielded to temptation. What consequences might have followed?

4. Can you give an example in your own life how the awareness of consequences for sexual sin has

prevented you from sinning?

5. Think about the consequences Samson suffered for his sin. Do you think he struggled with feeling the consequences were unfair?

6. How do people normally respond when they believe consequences are unfair?

7. Give an example of a "lightning-bolt" kind of consequence for sexual sin. (Try to draw from real life, not just a hypothetical situation.) Tell whether the consequence had a redemptive effect and why you think it did or did not have that effect.

RESPONSES ARE BASED ON ATTITUDES.

To understand our responses, we must know that actions and words (along with all the accompanying body language and non-verbal messages) ride on the attitudes and mind-set of the heart. Thus, it is not simply what we say or do that constitutes our response to situations, but the whole mental and emotional framework from which our words and actions come. In fact, although the words and actions are what others see (and often react to), the real culprit is the underlying attitude. To succeed in changing our responses, we must look at what drives them.

To better understand this, let's examine some wrong attitudes and contrast them with right attitudes. Then we will consider how these attitudes come out in words and actions.

WRONG ATTITUDES VS. RIGHT ATTITUDES

1. If I have repented, people should treat me fairly. *Right attitude: In my sexual sins, I have treated others unfairly,*

and I can expect that others may react by treating me unfairly.

2. When I repent, my sin is in the past and should be forgotten. *Right attitude: If what I have done creates ongoing sorrow or difficulty for others, it is right for me to take ongoing responsibility for my actions.*

3. My church and family are obligated to forgive me, which means everything should go on as before. *Right attitude: Forgiveness is an act of mercy, and although I can ask for it, I cannot demand it, even from Christians. Furthermore, when forgiveness is extended to me, it does not undo all the damage I have done to others, nor does it rebuild my character.*

4. If I have repented, people should trust me. *Right attitude: Where I have ruined my integrity and destroyed trust, I must take the responsibility to rebuild what I have damaged, no matter how long it takes.*

5. If I have repented, I should not have to face legal charges for illegal actions. *Right attitude: The forgiveness of God saves me from eternal punishment, but it does not give me freedom from legal consequences. If I must suffer as a lawbreaker, I should do it quietly and meekly.*

6. If someone turns me in to the law for illegal sexual conduct, he is ruining my reputation. *Right attitude: I have ruined my own reputation, and I will only make matters worse by blaming others.*

7. In trying to rebuild my life, people expect me to be perfect; any mistake I make is thrown against me. *Right attitude: I need the help and input of others to keep me accountable, so I don't even start down the wrong road.*

8. Confessing my sin only brought more trouble; it would have been better just to have confessed it to God. *Right attitude: Confessing my sin showed the true nature of sexual sin—that it hurts many people and has damaged my life. It is far better to face the consequences of confessed sin than the consequences of unconfessed sin.*

9. I can't go public with my confession because I would lose my reputation (or my position), and it would destroy my family. *Right attitude: The confession of my sin needs to be as public as the involvement of my sin. If sexual sin would disqualify me from what I am doing (were it known), a confession only reveals the truth that my sin has disqualified me. Confession does not ruin anyone's reputation; it is the first step in rebuilding a reputation of integrity.*

These attitudes often feed each other. Once we begin to think life is unfair or that people are being unfair, we can find a host of evidence to support our viewpoint. And the attitude sours into bitterness. We think about the unfairness. The more we think about it, the stronger we feel about it. Our attitude begins to show. Even when we say very little, our attitude becomes apparent through our facial expressions, our body language, and our whole disposition.

Of course, a healthy attitude is the same way. The more we think rightly, the easier it is to think more right thoughts. As we cultivate humble, meek, penitent, and gracious heart attitudes, the more those attitudes find expression in the way we relate to people and situations.

We referred to Shimei's hateful and unfair words and actions toward David. Since we have looked at the importance of attitudes, let's see how David responded. Keep in mind that this was at an extremely low point in David's life—he was fleeing from Jerusalem because his son Absalom had taken over the throne. Pay special attention to David's attitude.

> And when king David came to Bahurim, behold, thence came out a man of the family of the house of Saul, whose name was Shimei, the son of Gera: he came forth, and cursed still as he came. And he cast stones at David, and at all the servants of king David: and all the people and all the mighty men were on his right hand and on his left. And thus said Shimei when he cursed, Come out, come out, thou bloody man, and thou man of Belial: The LORD hath returned upon thee all the blood of the house of Saul, in whose stead thou hast reigned; and the LORD hath delivered the kingdom into the hand of Absalom thy son: and, behold, thou art taken in thy mischief, because thou art a bloody man.
>
> Then said Abishai the son of Zeruiah unto the king, Why should this dead dog curse my lord the king? let me go over, I pray thee, and take off his head. And the king said, What have I to do with you, ye sons of Zeruiah? so let him curse, because the LORD hath said unto him, Curse David. Who shall then say, Wherefore hast thou done so? And David said to Abishai, and to all his servants, Behold, my son, which came forth of my bowels, seeketh my life: how much more now may this Benjamite do it? let him alone, and let him curse; for the LORD hath bidden him. It may be that the LORD will look on mine affliction, and that the LORD will requite me good for his cursing this day. And as David and his men went by the way, Shimei went along on the hill's side over against him, and cursed as he went, and threw stones at him, and cast dust. 2 Samuel 16:5-13

HOW DO ATTITUDES DEVELOP?

Attitudes are settled ways of thinking and feeling. This means they start with a thought and they are fed by similar thoughts. As the thought patterns develop and grow, they begin to be accompanied by feelings until the whole mixture settles into a mind-set. This mind-set becomes the "front office" of the heart that screens all incoming and outgoing messages, and people who interact with our front office soon realize we have an attitude—we see everything from a particular viewpoint and we convey that viewpoint in whatever we say or do.

An attitude can be carried with us from one situation to another, or it may show itself in only one part of our lives. A young person, resentful because he is not allowed to do certain things, may carry that attitude from home to school and on to church. Or he may develop a bad attitude about taking orders. In most of life's situations, he shows a good attitude, but when told to do something (even when someone suggests he do something), he quickly shows a bad attitude.

So we might say that an attitude develops out of our thinking. Think a bad thought, and soon it can grow into a bad attitude. Think a good thought, and it, too, can grow into a good attitude.

But there is a deeper level to look at as well. Where do our thoughts come from? Can we just think a thought and it will become an attitude?

Jesus said our thoughts, like our words and our actions, come from our hearts (see Matthew 15:19). So it is the condition of the heart, even more than the nature of a thought, that determines the kind of attitudes we will have.

This is why penitence is so important in dealing with sin. If you look at the list of right attitudes given earlier, you will see that all of them reflect a broken, contrite heart. A person struggling with wrong attitudes in response to consequences cannot "grow" good attitudes unless the soil of his heart is right. If he allows the "unfairness" of the consequences to harden his heart, nothing but weeds will grow. But if, like David, he allows that unfairness to soften his heart—if he consciously turns to God in trust, in worship, in gratitude, and in humility—his heart will become fertile ground for healthy attitudes to grow. He can plant right thoughts in his mind, and they will grow into right attitudes.

And if this same person has a bad thought—a thought of self-pity or resentment or anger about his "rights"—the thought doesn't have a good chance of growing in his heart. He is accustomed to trusting God, being grateful for God's mercy, and humbly submitting to what God allows in his life. In that heart, the thought of self-pity or resentment soon withers. It simply can't take root in a heart that exercises regular and genuine fellowship with God.

So if we want right attitudes, we need right hearts. How are our hearts shaped rightly? More than any other way, they are shaped by the time we spend with God. If we want hearts that are tender and good, we must look regularly and long into the face of God. "But we all, with open face beholding as in a glass the glory of the Lord, are changed into the same image from glory to glory, even as by the Spirit of the Lord" (2 Corinthians 3:18). Right attitudes are formed, then, by seeking God's forgiveness, by praying for His grace to shape our lives, by seeking His guidance, by worshiping Him in gratitude and humility, and by building a close and meaningful relationship with Him.

FOR FURTHER STUDY:

1. Of the wrong attitudes listed, choose one you think is especially dangerous and tell why you think it is so.

2. List additional wrong attitudes you have had or have seen in others dealing with the consequences of sexual sin. For each one you list, write out what would be the right attitude.

3. Look up each of the following verses, and tell what attitude is reflected: a. Levi and Simeon, Genesis 34:31; b. Potiphar's wife, Genesis 38:13-18; c. David, 2 Samuel 16:9-12

4. Write the definition for *attitude*.

5. Although the word "attitude" is not found in the Bible (KJV), the concept is there. What attitude did Jesus have, according to Philippians 2:5, ff?

6. How are attitudes formed?

7. In your own life, what unhealthy attitude has been most troublesome? What steps might you take to work on this attitude?

8. Find additional verses that show that the heart is the source of thoughts, feelings, and attitudes.

9. If God is the primary shaper of a right heart, what are some practical ways to seek God?

10. What additional (or secondary) factors are involved in shaping the heart? For example, how do friends shape the heart? Can you support your answers with Scripture?

HOW DO ATTITUDES DRIVE RESPONSES?

Let's carry this forward now, and explore how attitudes drive our responses. We will look first at wrong responses and then consider right responses.

WRONG RESPONSES:

When we have wrong attitudes, we say and do all sorts of things that add to the problem and increase the consequences. Unfortunately, people involved in immoral actions and relationships often go to great lengths to try to protect their reputation, to avoid the consequences for their sin, and to coerce others to cooperate with them. This is the worst route to take. It demonstrates that the transgressor is still self-seeking, unwilling to face the full truth of his sin, and in need of true brokenness.

These are some of the ways wrong attitudes drive one's words and actions:

1. Pointing out how wrong others are in their responses.
2. Demanding forgiveness or accusing people of not forgiving.
3. Criticizing leaders or family members for how they handle the situation.
4. Playing on sympathies: "You will ruin me."
5. Threatening or bargaining to get people to cooperate.
6. Giving gifts or donations to obligate people to cooperate.
7. Pressuring people to promise to be silent about the sin.
8. Complaining about rumors.
9. Accusing people of "digging up the past."
10. Minimizing the sin or its consequences.
11. Accusing others of wrong motives for being involved.
12. Blowing up, glaring, pouting, or otherwise intimidating people.

These responses only make a bad situation worse. People do not trust a defensive person. They find it hard to accept a testimony of deliverance from a person who is demanding forgiveness. They easily doubt the depth of repentance when a person refuses to talk about certain issues, tries to control what others are saying, and complains about how he is being treated.

What a difference it makes when a transgressor is truly broken, has a humble attitude about himself, and is willing to do whatever is required instead of trying to force others to cooperate with him! There is hope and help for the brokenhearted.

RIGHT RESPONSES:

So how do we respond in ways that will help resolve the issues? Again, the *attitude* we have is fundamental to all our responses. When our eyes are on God, we can respond properly to people. Although we cannot describe right responses to every kind of situation, here are a few examples:

1. Confessing sin clearly and without excuse, especially to those who have been hurt by the sin.
2. Taking responsibility for sin without making excuses or implicating others.
3. Doing whatever possible to bring healing and help to those who have been hurt.
4. Accepting injustice meekly—that is, with humility, recognizing it as part of the price of sin.
5. Asking for forgiveness, and receiving it as undeserved.
6. Accepting any refusal to forgive without complaint.
7. Being understanding of those who are angered or embittered by the sin.
8. Expressing gratitude to those who attempt to help,

even when their help seems inconvenient or insensitive.

9. Cooperating with those responsible to deal with the sin (pastors, law officers, or family leaders).
10. Agreeing with those who denounce the sin.
11. Acknowledging the ways this sin has made things difficult for others.
12. Asking for prayer in the struggle to rebuild character.
13. Giving people the benefit of the doubt when they misunderstand or misrepresent the situation.
14. Refusing the urge to engage in self-justification.
15. When falsely or harshly accused, asking the Lord to bring about a heart tenderness and humility before Him.

The person who humbly accepts responsibility for his sin and seeks God fervently, stands in a good position to respond correctly. As pride serves to stir up conflict, even so, humility tends to calm tense situations and soften strong feelings. A humble, penitent person is far more likely to be believed than the person who is closed, complaining, or reactive.

FOR FURTHER STUDY:

1. Describe a situation in your own life where a wrong response made consequences worse. Describe a situation where a right response to consequences helped to calm the tension.
2. Looking at the list of wrong responses, identify the ones you struggle with personally. Then as accurately as you can, describe the attitude(s) reflected by those responses.

3. Look again at the account of David and Shimei (2 Samuel 16:5-13). What do you find exemplary about David's attitude in this time when he was experiencing consequences for his sin? (If you have trouble, review the list of right responses we just looked at, and identify those David demonstrated.)

4. How do you think David's life would have been different had he shown a wrong attitude?

5. What do you think is the tie between what we read in Psalm 51 and the attitude David demonstrated here?

6. How do you think David's attitude and responses affected those following him?

7. From the list of right responses, which do you most admire? Which would you personally find most difficult?

RESPONDING TO CONSEQUENCES IN ONE'S FAMILY.

Some of the most painful and confusing consequences for sexual sins occur in one's family. As seen in the life of David, sexual sin seems to open the next generation to special temptations. Just to review these: 1) David's son Amnon laid a trap and then forced David's daughter Tamar to have sex. 2) Later, Absalom had sexual relations with some of David's servant wives, purposely to shame David.

What can parents do to avoid unnecessary consequences in their children?

In the case of David's children, a lack of communication on David's part may well have contributed to the problem. Children may have a variety of responses to sexual sins in their parents—shame, disgust, or anger. But typically, they are not indifferent, even though they may appear to be so. We are not told how Amnon or Absalom felt about David's sin with

Bathsheba. In the Biblical record, we simply have the sad story of David's sin, followed by the even sadder story of Amnon's sin. Did David's sin embolden Amnon to sin? We are not told directly.

When Amnon forced Tamar, however, we are told that David was very angry, and also that Absalom was very angry. David did not hide his anger, but Absalom apparently did. "And Absalom spake unto his brother Amnon neither good nor bad: for Absalom hated Amnon, because he had forced his sister Tamar" (2 Samuel 13:22).

Although David was extremely upset in this situation, we have no record that he attempted to help either Amnon or Absalom—or Tamar, for that matter. He took no judicial action against Amnon. Absalom cared for Tamar; that is, she went to live in his house. And David did virtually nothing.

We could well wonder how the chain of events might have been altered if David had communicated with Absalom at this point. Absalom might have refused to talk, so great was his hatred for Amnon. But if David had invited Absalom to talk about how Amnon's sin affected him, encouraged him to face his anger and hatred, and urged him to open his bitter heart to the Lord, would Absalom have chosen a different path?

Instead, we see David and Absalom mourning for their losses separately and walking separate roads in their recovery. Three years after the death of Amnon, David's heart is turning toward Absalom again, but when Joab arranged for Absalom to return home, David stiffened his heart and said, "Let him turn to his own house, and let him not see my face" (2 Samuel 14:24). As if this were not enough, David continued to hold his son at a distance. "So Absalom dwelt two full years in Jerusalem, and saw not the king's face" (v. 28).

We might speculate about David's motives, but we are not

told clearly. Did he think Absalom's decision to take vengeance into his own hands deserved punishment? Was he afraid of Absalom? Did he fear that opening himself to Absalom would reveal too much of his own heart? Or was he simply like many males today, afraid that showing his emotions would make him too vulnerable? We don't know. But clearly, the walls David built wrecked what relationship there was between him and Absalom. Some of the consequences in David's family seem to have been brought on by David's attitudes and the resulting actions.

By the end of those two years of purposeful distance from his father, Absalom was seething. "Wherefore am I come from Geshur? it had been good for me to have been there still: now therefore let me see the king's face; and if there be any iniquity in me, let him kill me" (2 Samuel 14:32).

We can suggest a number of guidelines based on this account:

1. A person who has been immoral should establish and maintain open communication with his family. (The openness should be appropriate to the age of the children, of course.)

2. Being publicly penitent does not substitute for private penitence before one's companion and children.

3. The children of an immoral person will have struggles as a result of the immorality, and parents are a necessary part of working through those struggles.

4. Part of working through those struggles includes letting the child verbalize his deep feelings, including feelings of anger, bitterness, or hatred. (I am not advocating mere "venting" of feelings. But we can seldom point an angry person toward forgiveness and faith unless we have the courage to hear him out.)

5. One of God's appointed ways for us to connect with our children is in their distresses (even as He connects with us). Where our sin has distressed our children, we must have the courage to invite them to us.

6. When our children use our sin as a screen for their own sin, we must not build walls in our relationship. Distance only increases anger. Honesty and humility and penitence can restore connection.

7. We must be sensitive to the right timing to talk to our children. Sometimes this is a matter of age—young children are not ready to hear about it, and even adolescents may not be prepared to talk about it. But we must build and then maintain the kind of open relationship with our children that, when the time is right, they can talk. As we observe in Absalom, there is clearly a time when talking is too late. After the two years of purposeful distance, the opportunity for David to reach Absalom was likely past. There is a time when children are not ready, and there is a time when it is too late. Somewhere between, there is a right time to talk.

8. Pastors (or other helpers) should work to enable communication and relationship between parents and their children. A pastor can fill a vital role in families where trust has been broken. A pastor can even, to some extent, fill in for an immoral father, but he can never replace him. The pastor should, in fact, guard against replacing the role of the father. In David's case, Ahithophel took the role of Absalom's counselor, doing only greater damage to the relationship.

SUMMARY

The man or woman who becomes ensnared in immorality will face consequences. He who truly repents needs much wisdom and grace to respond correctly in the time that follows repentance. The broken heart, the open heart, the humble and sincere heart is prepared to respond correctly. With right responses, the person who has repented of immorality will find that the consequences actually move him closer to God. His tender heart will remain tender through the pain and the difficulties that follow his immorality. This will be a time of growth, a time of healing, and a time of rebuilding trust with his family and church people.

FOR FURTHER STUDY:

1. What struggles do children commonly face when one or both of their parents have been immoral?

2. If a guilty parent is defensive or bitter about how he has been treated, how does this affect the children?

3. List some practical ways parents can establish openness with their children.

4. Suppose a teenager is obviously angry about what his parents have done, but he refuses to talk to them. What are some approaches that could enable the child to face his anger?

5. What are some things parents should not do?

6. What are some pointers for a pastor who wishes to help rebuild communication between parents and their estranged children? What are some things a pastor should avoid?

7. What are the results of attempting to push a child to talk about his or her thoughts and feelings before the

child is ready to talk?

8. How does the account of Absalom show that God holds grown children responsible, even when their parents have failed?

9. What are some tactful ways to guide grown children to face their responsibilities even when their (unfaithful) parents have hindered communication?

10. What are right attitudes for grown children to have in response to unfaithful parents?

7

LIVING A PURE LIFE

"Wherewithal shall a young man
cleanse his way?
by taking heed thereto according to thy word.
With my whole heart have I sought thee:
O let me not wander from thy commandments."
Psalm 119:9, 10

"Blessed are the pure in heart:
for they shall see God."
Matthew 5:8

We live in a fallen world. Sexual sin has always been a problem and always will be, no matter what culture we live in. Obviously, some cultures are looser in their standards, and cultures shift over time. Western culture has been shifting toward Sodom for many years, and with the lifting of the Iron Curtain in the twentieth century, many former Communist countries have joined the slide.

To be serious about following God in any culture at any time calls for courage and character. To live this way in a rotting culture takes special grace. Peter reports that Lot was "vexed with the filthy conversation of the wicked: (For that righteous man dwelling among them, in seeing and hearing, vexed his righteous soul from day to day with their unlawful deeds)" (2 Peter 2:7, 8).

The practical question is this: How does a godly man or woman live a pure life in a morally perverted culture? Besides being "vexed" or spiritually distressed by the sin around us, how can we stand straight, walk straight, and live straight day by day when the pressures are to bend and twist and pervert pure thinking and pure living?

Paul's letter to the Romans provides practical help for us. "The night is far spent, the day is at hand: let us therefore cast off the works of darkness, and let us put on the armour of light. Let us walk honestly, as in the day; not in rioting and drunkenness, not in chambering and wantonness, not in strife and envying. But put ye on the Lord Jesus Christ, and make not provision for the flesh, to fulfill the lusts thereof" (Romans 13:12-14).

From this Scripture, we will look at three practical principles for living a pure life.

WE MUST WALK IN LIGHT.

In the Scriptures, light and darkness are constantly set in contrast to each other, not simply as night and day, but symbolically as good and evil. "God is light," John declares, "and in him is no darkness at all" (1 John 1:5). In following God, we are called to "walk in the light, as he is in the light" (1 John 1:7). God's Word is a "lamp" that brings "light" to our paths (see Psalm 119:105). Jesus said, "I am the light of the world: he that followeth me shall not walk in darkness, but shall have the light of life" (John 8:12). He is called the "true Light, which lighteth every man that cometh into the world" (John 1:9). Paul says of us, "For ye were sometimes darkness, but now are ye light in the Lord." And he adds, "Walk as children of light. And have no fellowship with the unfruitful works of darkness, but rather reprove them" (Ephesians 5:8, 11). Furthermore, the celestial city toward which we yearn, has "no need of the sun, neither of the moon, to shine in it: for the glory of God did lighten it, and the Lamb is the light thereof. And there shall be no night there; and they need no candle, neither light of the sun; for the Lord God giveth them light" (Revelation 21:23; 22:5).

So when Paul instructs us to "cast off the works of darkness" and to "put on the armour of light," we understand that he is talking about good and evil. We are to fling off evil thoughts and actions, and clothe ourselves with thoughts and actions of truth and righteousness. What does this mean?

1. *Putting on the armor of light means we do right things and think right things.* "Let us walk honestly [or honorably], as in the day" he says, (Romans 13:13). We are to do what is commendable and aboveboard, things we would be unashamed for anyone to know about. The older English "honest" is what we think of today as "noble" or "venerable."

To "walk honorably" is to treat the opposite sex with respect. For a man, this means to look a lady in the face, instead of inspecting her figure. It means thinking of her as a person with thoughts and feelings and problems and goals, not as simply a sexual being. It means thinking of her as having an eternal soul who will someday stand before God, rather than an object to be used for personal pleasure.

To "walk honorably" means to respect the privacy of others, to maintain healthy boundaries in interaction with the opposite sex. It means avoiding emotionally intimate conversations that build secret bonds. It means treating older women as we would want our mother to be treated and treating younger women as we would want our sisters to be treated and treating young girls as we would want our daughters to be treated (see 1 Timothy 5:2). It means being discreet in touch practices between the sexes, cultivating touch practices even in our families and extended families that are honorable and appropriate to the level of relationship, and that do not create embarrassment or stir sensual thoughts. It means structuring dating activities and establishing touch boundaries in courtship so that both partners can stand pure and unashamed at the wedding altar.

To "walk honorably" means to avoid exposing the lady's figure or the man's body in ways that stir sensual thoughts. It means being discreet in teasing and joking between the sexes, keeping humor healthy and aboveboard. It means dads treating their daughters with respect, and young men treating their mothers and sisters with respect. It means parents protecting the innocence of their children and guiding their adolescents through their sexual development—not teasing children about love affairs or making jokes about their sexuality.

To live this way is to live with moral protection. It is the armor of light, the protection of moral uprightness. Men and women who live this way may still be tempted, they may still face pressure to conform to the sensual lifestyles around them, but they are less likely to yield to temptation. Their minds are set on living differently. They have the protection of high moral standards. The "breastplate of righteousness" guards their hearts. They are not perfect. They do not walk with their noses in the air. But they are not ashamed to do right and think right, whether alone or in the company of others.

2. Putting on the "armor of light" means cultivating openness.

We are to live the kind of life, in other words, that would be open to inspection at any time. Jesus said, "He that doeth truth cometh to the light, that his deeds may be made manifest, that they are wrought in God" (John 3:21). The man or woman who has been involved in sexual sin and who is committed to living a morally pure life needs to give special attention to cultivating openness. We can do this "on purpose." That is, we can invite other believers to regularly observe our lives, ask us questions about our activities, and know what is truly going on at any time in our lives.

Practicing this kind of openness is altogether different from the covering, hiding disposition of those who walk in darkness. Jesus said of them, "Every one that doeth evil hateth the light, neither cometh to the light, lest his deeds should be reproved" (John 3:20). One of the sure signs of repentance from sexual sin and commitment to lead a pure life is the change from hiding patterns to patterns of openness. When we want to "cast off the works of darkness," when we are truly done with masturbation, pornography, flirting, and unfaithfulness, we seek to "walk in the light." We want our actions to be open before the people who care most about, and are most affected by, the true nature of our hearts. We invite questions. We ask for checkpoints.

Walking in the day is protection for us. It is spiritual protection against the snares of the flesh, the world, and the evil one. Sin must have covers to thrive. It thrives when it is protected from light. Excuses and lies and pretense give sexual sin freedom to multiply.

Light is death to sin. The person who is serious about changing immoral behavior to morally upright behavior must change from covering his actions to exposing them. Living in the light, giving his sins no cover, inviting the right people to know what he does at any time of the day or night gives him protection from sin's power and is helpful in turning from sin to righteousness.

Practical ways to cultivate openness include:

- Asking a trusted friend to check on me regularly with key questions.
- Setting aside time to talk to my companion about troublesome issues, inviting him/her to ask questions.
- Reporting on time spent in "dangerous" areas, or having someone go with me. (Examples of danger zones could be going to town or traveling alone or working on a computer.)
- Asking several key friends to pray for me about specific issues I face, or alerting them to times I may be tempted.
- Making a commitment that if I fail, I will acknowledge it that same day to a companion or accountability person.
- Acknowledging my problem areas to my congregation. "Confess your faults one to another, and pray one for another, that ye may be healed" (James 5:16).

Now a balancing word. Openness does not mean spilling out the contents of our hearts to anyone who will listen. It does not mean walking around with our hearts turned inside out. With openness, especially about struggles with impure thoughts and actions, there is the balancing principle of discretion. We need to be open with the right people, the people in our lives to whom our moral purity matters. For young people, this would mean their parents. For a married person, this would include his/her companion. For a church member, this means brothers and sisters—again, as it is proper for the relationship. A public confession needs to be clear enough that people know how to pray, but not so detailed that it pollutes people's minds. Some things done in secret are "a shame to speak of" in public settings (Ephesians 5:12).

FOR FURTHER STUDY:

1. List the two dimensions to "walking in the light."
2. In practical ways, tell what it means for men to relate to women "honorably."
3. In practical ways, tell what it means for women to relate to men "honorably."
4. Younger people sometimes think the older generation was not open enough, and older people sometimes think the younger generation is too open. Tell how each may be right.
5. What is the value of being open with someone about sexual temptation and sin?
6. What criteria should we use to select someone with whom to be open about our sexual temptations and failures?
7. In practical terms, describe what "openness" should mean for each of the following people: a. An 18-year-old young man living at home. b. A 25-year-old single lady living alone. c. A father who often travels alone. d. A married lady whose husband is passive and spiritually shallow and who finds herself attracted to spiritually mature men. e. A man whose job requires the use of a computer with Internet service. f. A married man who has struggled with pornography and masturbation.
8. Choose one or two of the above people and list several ways openness could be carried beyond what is healthy.

9. Why is it that some people need more openness than others in the area of their sexuality? Do you think this is fair or unfair?

WE MUST "CLOTHE OURSELVES" WITH THE LORD JESUS CHRIST.

This is the second instruction given by Paul at the close of Romans 13. We are to "put on the armour of light" (v. 12) and we are likewise to "put ye on the Lord Jesus Christ" (v. 14) What does this mean?

To live a pure life in a morally corrupt society, we need the lordship and presence of Jesus. Let's start with looking at His lordship.

After Jesus was raised from the dead by the power of God, He was seated at the right hand of God, "far above all principality, and power, and might, and dominion, and every name that is named, not only in this world, but also in that which is to come" (Ephesians 1:21). Jesus has position like no other. He has authority like no other. He has a title like no other. He is Lord *over all*.

When Jesus commanded sickness to leave, it left. When He commanded the wind to quiet down, it calmed. When He commanded water to become wine, it changed instantly. When He declared sins forgiven, they were wiped away. When He told evil spirits to be gone, they left—shrieking. This is *lordship*. And lordship is inherent in Jesus—He IS Lord, and He is absolute Lord. He can be no other.

Now let's think about sin. One of the characteristics of sin is that it brings the sinner into bondage. Sins of the flesh seem to be especially binding. They ensnare the mind, making it captive and pulling the sinner back again and again to do the same sin over and over, even after he is sick of it. Thus, the psalmist prays, "Order my steps in thy word: and let not any iniquity have dominion over me" (Psalm 119:133). The nature of sin is to dominate, to put into bondage, to rob the sinner of moral strength, so that even when he knows what he is doing is destructive, he is powerless to change.

Deliverance from sexual sin comes through the lordship of Jesus. "Clothe yourselves with the Lord Jesus Christ," Paul advises. That is, surround your body with the mantle of Jesus. He is Lord. He cannot be "put under," for He is above all. When His lordship is over us, He can speak the word that breaks the power of sin. When He commands, none can resist His Word. Sin cannot abide (live as a resident) in the heart that is fully under the lordship of Jesus.

How does this happen?

There are no formulas that can bring us under the lordship of Jesus. The heart must break, surrender—yield with no conditions and nothing held back. When we unite in our hearts with the Lord of All, He can break the power of sin in our lives. He may do this in different ways for different people and different situations. But He is Lord, and sin must yield to His authority.

Richard Mummau was an alcoholic for many years. He left his wife because of his drinking. He was so addicted that he could not function until he had alcohol of some kind in his system. The day he decided to go for help, he stopped at a bar to get a drink so he could sign his name for some last-minute business. Several weeks later, in the process of "drying out," Richard was asked to sign a statement of absolute surrender to Jesus. Here is a copy:

My Covenant

Lord, I give up all my own plans and purposes, all my own desires and hopes, and accept Thy will for my life. I give myself, my life, my all utterly to Thee to be Thine forever. Fill me with Thy Holy Spirit. Use me as Thou wilt: send me where Thou wilt: work out Thy whole will in my life at any cost, now and forever.

Signed: _____

Date: _____

Knowing what it would mean for him to sign, Richard carried that covenant around for several days before he actually signed it. But his testimony was that signing that statement of surrender was the decisive turning point for him. From that day onward, he was delivered from the power of strong drink.[1]

Sins of the flesh are powerful—they have turned many strong men into weak captives, led around by their lusts. But the authority of the Lord Jesus is stronger still. Sins of the flesh must yield to Jesus when we clothe ourselves with Him.

FOR FURTHER STUDY:

1. Why is it that we need the lordship of Jesus to overcome sin? List as many reasons as you can, supporting your answers from the Bible.

2. From the New Testament, give an example of Jesus demonstrating His lordship. What or who yielded to His lordship?

3. Read 1 Corinthians 12:3. Who stands ready to enable us to confess the lordship of Jesus?

4. Have you confessed the lordship of Jesus over your sexuality? Is there any area of your sexual thoughts or activities that is not under His lordship? To assess this, consider the following areas: thought life, humor, touch practices, sharing with the opposite sex, eye habits, appearance, music, videos, radio or TV programs. If any of these areas regularly trip you up, tell honestly how it does so, and then tell what you could do about it.2

5. Write out a confession of Jesus' lordship for your sexuality, asking the Holy Spirit to guide your words and to address specific areas of weakness. Then follow up with these steps:

   a. Read this confession daily until you experience a change.

   b. Ask Jesus to direct your ways, and write down anything He tells you to do or any inspiration He gives that encourages you.

CULTIVATING RELATIONSHIP WITH JESUS.

Paul's instruction is to "put on" or "clothe" ourselves with Jesus. We clothe our bodies daily. Putting on our clothes is a regular and natural part of living. We don't start the duties of the day without clothing ourselves.

Paul says we are to clothe ourselves with Jesus—He is to be a regular and natural part of our living. How do we do this?

1. To clothe ourselves with Jesus means daily receiving from Him. The "clothing" analogy speaks to how regular and natural the presence of Jesus should be in our lives, but it doesn't describe how our interaction with Him works. Other analogies in the Bible explain our interaction with Jesus.

Jesus spoke of our relationship as that of a vine and its

branches. We are joined to Him in a living union. He is our life. He is our nourishment. We continually absorb spiritual vitality from Him. Whatever we do, we do in union with Him, seeking strength, courage, direction, and wisdom from Him. When we face a decision, we ask Him. When we face temptation, we call out to Him. When we are asked to do something, we depend on Him. We draw from Jesus in everything we do. In every responsibility, in every place, at all times we are conscious that Jesus is with us according to His promise. "If a man love me, he will keep my words: and my Father will love him, and we will come unto him, and make our abode with him" (John 14:23). "For without me ye can do nothing" (John 15:5).

Some people, perhaps with the intent to magnify Jesus, have de-emphasized our involvement. One hymn writer speaks of us, for example, as "channels only." We are the channels, the vessels, the vehicles by which Jesus lives His life through us. In this analogy, however, the believer is basically uninvolved—no volition, no thought, no action, indeed, no life. He thinks of himself as a pipeline, wanting Jesus to do whatever He purposes. Of course, in actual living, most believers realize they must say the words or do the deeds Jesus would have them do. The vine analogy is far better—the branches are alive, and they bear fruit. Their life and vitality come from the vine, but they are vitally involved in living and producing fruit. For us, this means we should not try to quit thinking or quit deciding or quit purposing, but to think and decide and purpose with the life and presence of Jesus fully alive within us.

Another analogy, even closer to our actual experience is the analogy of the body. Jesus is the Head, and we are the members of His body. To have Jesus living in us means He is imparting life, He is giving direction, He is urging us and sharing with us His wisdom and strength and purpose. These "living" analogies suggest, however, that we also are alive and actively involved in the doing and saying and purposing. Fellowship with Jesus does not obliterate who we are. It is so radically different from our life without Jesus that we can speak of the change as a "new birth" and refer to the "old man" who has died and the "new man" who now has Jesus living within. But the new person is very much alive and growing and becoming the unique member of His body Jesus intended him to be.

2. *To clothe ourselves with Jesus means to talk and interact with Him.* As already implied, our relationship with Jesus is not just one of receiving. Even as we regularly draw from Him, we also are regularly giving back to Him. We give Him thanks, adoration, and honor. We tell Him audibly and in our spirit what He means to us. We praise His works. We express our appreciation. We worship Him.

We can do this in song. We can break out in joyful expression, "Thank You, Jesus!" We can tell others. And we can silently contemplate.

Our world is full of things, people, business, busyness, appointments, coming, and going. It is healthy to take time for solitude with Jesus, even as He often took time to be alone with His Father. In those times of solitude, we may meditate on such wonderful aspects of our relationship as His forgiveness of our sins, the means of that forgiveness (His death), His present work for us in Heaven, or some part of His earthly ministry. In that quiet time of contemplation, we can worship Him, thank Him, let our hearts fill with adoration, and express that adoration whether in words or "in the Spirit" beyond words.

Taking time to fellowship with Jesus is essential to clothing ourselves with His presence. Walking with Jesus is not just a spiritual phrase. It is intended to be a living reality. Jesus is a real person. He is fully alive. It is right to think of Him with us everywhere we go. It is right to speak to Him and listen to His voice no matter what we are doing. This is what a Christian is—one who follows Jesus, one who is in constant communion with Him in spirit.

Those who clothe themselves with Jesus will find Him a mighty presence against sin. In union with Jesus, they will find that sin loses its power. The temptations of the flesh are powerful when we are on our own, but when we cultivate living, real, regular communion with Jesus, sin must yield. When temptation comes at us, the presence of Jesus rises up with a divine NO to sin. This voice is not against us (don't you dare to sin), but rather it is against sin, against Satan, against the world. Never! Get out of here! Those who live in union with Jesus and experience this divine "rising up" within them when they are tempted are delighted and blessed.

A man who is walking with Jesus (praising Him in his spirit, thanking Him for who He is and what He has done, and drawing from Him for wisdom) is not above temptation. He may see a beautiful woman—shapely and immodestly dressed. The sight of this woman may stir desire, and suddenly, he senses the holiness within rising up. There is a divine authority that says, "Absolutely not! She does not belong to you." And immediately that man can think of her as a person—a woman with needs like every other human being, a person who will someday stand before the Lord of all the earth to give account for her life. Not only is this man experiencing the divine *no* against sin, but he is able to view people as Jesus sees them.

"Clothe yourselves," Paul says, "with Jesus!" Don't face one day, one situation, one temptation, one responsibility, without Him.

FOR FURTHER STUDY:

1. What do we receive in spiritual union with Jesus?
2. What do we give back in union with Jesus?
3. Describe the difference between the "channels only" understanding of our relationship with Jesus and the "vine and branch" understanding. How do you think the latter understanding affects our view of Jesus? How does it affect our view of ourselves?
4. Describe the "divine no" to sin (consider also Titus 2:11-13). Can you relate an incident in which you experienced the strength of Jesus against sin?
5. List some practical ways we "clothe" ourselves with Jesus.
6. List some of the ways we may be hindered in clothing ourselves with Jesus. How will understanding these hindrances help us?

WE MUST MAKE NO PROVISION FOR THE FLESH.

This is the third of Paul's instructions in Romans 13. "Put on the armour of light. Put ye on the Lord Jesus Christ, and make not provision for the flesh, to fulfil the lusts thereof" (Romans 13:12, 14).

The desires of the flesh are strong. When they are fed wrongly—that is, when we violate God's guidelines to satisfy bodily appetites—those desires increase to the point where they dominate the mind and will. Coming under the lordship of Jesus breaks the power of fleshly appetites that have gone berserk.

But we still must take precautions. By the power of Jesus, the flesh can be rendered powerless, and yet, the potential is always there for the flesh to revive if we yield to its desires. We must make absolutely no provision for those appetites to be satisfied in the old ways.

This calls for safeguards.

There is no universal set of safeguards against fleshly lusts, but some things are dangerous for anyone. Following is a list of ways men are led into sexual sins with women:

1. By listening to or using dirty language or telling off-color jokes.
2. By looking at immodestly dressed (or undressed) women, whether in magazines or real life.
3. By reading about (or watching) the passions of a woman.
4. By confiding in a woman or allowing a woman to confide in him.
5. By developing a close working relationship with a woman.
6. By text-messaging, emailing, or writing personal notes to a woman.
7. By ride-sharing with a woman.
8. By sharing personal items with a woman (coffee cup, eating utensils, jacket).
9. By excessive humor with a woman.
10. By playful or teasing touch.
11. By teasing a woman.
12. By effuse compliments to a woman.
13. By allowing emotional distance to build between him and his wife.
14. By two or more couples developing excessive and exclusive relationships.
15. By traveling alone.
16. By giving his best person (effort, time, and disposition) to his work.

For a woman, many of these things may be equally dangerous, but some danger areas for a woman will be the counterpart to the above. For example, she may be led into sexual sin by appearing or acting in provocative ways—using her eyes or her body or her laughter to attract the attentions of men. Or she may become needy (have a distressing problem, even create a problem) in the presence of a man she admires and look to him to resolve it.

For a person who wants to live a morally pure life, setting healthy standards of behavior and speech and interaction with the opposite sex is integral to making no provision for the flesh. We must intentionally keep ourselves from temptation.

But beyond this, every man or woman who has been sexually loose will have particular weak areas and weak times, and particular circumstances that are perilous. Before setting safeguards, therefore, it is wise to discern the specific avenues through which a person was led into sin. In assessing these, we must realize that what is dangerous for one person may not be for another. We must also understand that safeguards against specific weaknesses are not placed between what is right and wrong so much as between what is safe and what is not safe. What would have been perfectly fine had it not been for indulgence, in other words, can become unsafe for the person who sinned.

A common example is that of a drunkard accustomed to going to a particular bar. After he is delivered from strong drink, he might set the safeguard that he will not drive down that particular street. Driving down that street is not wrong, but for that man, it is unsafe. Others might drive down that street without a temptation, but not the man who has worn a path to that particular bar. Similarly, if a man or woman is more tempted to masturbate at a particular time of day or in a particular location or in a particular set of circumstances or under the influence of a particular frame of mind, he or she will wisely consider what kinds of safeguards will help to avoid stirring that temptation. As Alcorn says, *"It's a sin to deliberately put ourselves in a position where we'll likely commit sin"* [emphasis his].[3]

We must note here that no safeguards will help if Paul's first two instructions are not heeded. When the heart is not fully set to do right (putting on the armor of light), or when the power of the Lord Jesus is not present (clothing ourselves with the Lord Jesus), setting safeguards will only serve to make the flesh more subtle and more determined to have its way. The strength of man is not sufficient to tame the inflamed desires of the flesh. Rules from the outside in won't control lusts accustomed to getting what they want. "Touch not; taste not; handle not . . . which things have indeed a show of wisdom in will-worship, and humility, and neglecting of the body; not in any honour to the satisfying of the flesh." Or as the NIV says, "Such regulations indeed have an appearance of wisdom, with their self-imposed worship, their false humility and their harsh treatment of the body, but they lack any value in restraining sensual indulgence" (Colossians 2:23).

But when the heart is right and when the Lord Jesus is present, we are wise to take precautions against fleshly desires, especially those we have indulged in years past. Any man or woman who professes to have been delivered from the power of inflamed fleshly desires and who is careless about the old haunts of sin or bold to put himself or herself close to former sins is on dangerous ground. Rejoice in deliverance! Glory in the power of the Lord Jesus! But take heed to Paul's warning, *"Make not provision* for the flesh, to fulfill the lusts thereof!"

Here are examples of personal safeguards against sexual sins:

1. I will not go to town alone. (Or, when I go to town, I will report to my companion exactly where I've been and what I have done.)
2. I will not travel alone.
3. I will not talk to a person of the opposite sex alone (or to a particular person alone).
4. I will not carry a cell phone.
5. I will not use the computer except when family members are present.
6. I will not call the home of _____.
7. I will not go to a particular store.
8. When I find myself angry (or depressed), I will call _____.
9. I will not pick up the mail myself, and I will have someone assigned to purge the advertising fliers before I see them.
10. I will not read books written by _____. (Or I will designate someone to screen and approve any books I read.)
11. I will carry only a certain limit of cash and will not carry or use a credit card except by approval of _____.
12. I will not ride-share with a woman.
13. We will not have television in our home.
14. We will not vacation where there is public bathing.

Safeguards work best when they are written by (or at the request of) the person who needs them. They do not work as well when imposed on a person needing them. They must be the expression of a heart set on doing right and following Jesus, not simply the wishes of friends or family members. On the other hand, a person who is rebuilding trust with family or church members may voluntarily submit to safeguards that he may not see as necessary but that he realizes are important to others. By glad submission to the concerns of others, the offender is not only likely to rebuild trust, but may also be guarding himself against a danger of which he is not fully aware. Sometimes those around us know our weaknesses better than we do—such is the deceitfulness of the flesh.

As indicated in the list of safeguards, some dangers are in the physical/material world—that is, places, people, and activities. Other dangers exist in the less visible realm of our feelings. Some people are particularly vulnerable to sexual sins when they find themselves in a certain mood or state of mind. For some people, it is anger. For others, it may be discouragement or loneliness. For others, it is when people compliment them or make them feel important. To safeguard ourselves against the lusts of the flesh, we must know when and where and by what means those lusts are stimulated. Then we can take appropriate action.

No set of safeguards is foolproof. In other words, safeguards do not insure victory over the flesh, but they can help to avoid temptation.

SUMMARY

A morally pure life is a life worth living. Satan, the world, and the flesh would have us to think otherwise, that we are missing out on fun and excitement. That "fun and excitement," however, is always followed by overwhelming heartache (a heartache that effectively nullifies any former pleasure). But a person who lives a morally upright life has the joy of doing right, the deep-seated approval of his conscience, the respect of those around him, and the "well-done" of God Himself. "Blessed!" Jesus cried, "are the pure in heart: for they shall see

God" (Matthew 5:8).

FOR FURTHER STUDY:

1. List the three instructions Paul gives for living above sins of the flesh.
2. What dangers are associated with following the first two and neglecting the third?
3. What dangers are associated with trying to do the third without following the first two?
4. Why is it best for the person who needs these safeguards to set them up (or be involved in setting them up) rather than for someone else to impose them on him?
5. List some safeguards (either from the list or otherwise) that you have needed to set up to avoid yielding to sexual temptation.
6. Why is it important to have others involved in setting up safeguards?
7. If you have been under the bondage of a particular sexual sin, identify as clearly as possible the places, people, situations, activities, or moods where you find yourself most vulnerable.
8. Considering these danger areas, draw up a list of safeguards. Do this with the person(s) who will hold you responsible.
9. Suppose a wife thinks a safeguard for her husband is necessary, but her husband does not. How should this be resolved? What benefits might a husband reap by respecting his wife's concern?
10. What are the limitations of safeguards—that is, what can they do and what can they not do?

THE PROBLEM OF MASTURBATION

"For this is the will of God,
that you should be consecrated—
separated and set apart for
pure and holy living;
that you should abstain from all sexual vice;
that each one of you should know
how to possess [control, manage]
his own body
(in purity, separated from things profane, and)
in consecration and honor,
not [to be used] in the passion of lust,
like the heathen who are
ignorant of the true God
and have no knowledge of His will."
1 Thessalonians 4:3-5, Amplified[1]

I address the subject of masturbation in an appendix largely because it is more of an issue with some people than others. Not all readers will find this material necessary.

I will begin with several introductory thoughts on the subject, share my reasons for believing masturbation is wrong, address some of the problems that accompany masturbation, and then provide practical help for living above it. So let's begin with some opening statements.

1. This subject is controversial.

Some people, including some influential Christian teachers, view masturbation as neither a sin nor a significant problem. They do not necessarily encourage people to engage in masturbation, but they assume that many, especially adolescents, will. Because they see nothing physically or spiritually harmful in it, why make it an issue?

Others view masturbation as wrong. They see it as an activity contrary to God's purpose, and therefore, when a person sexually stimulates himself, his activity is sinful. They believe the proper response for a Christian who engages in this activity is to repent.

2. Masturbation is not just a male problem, but typically there are differences in the issues surrounding masturbation for a man as compared to a woman.

Although men seem to struggle with masturbation more commonly than women, some women also masturbate. Young single men probably have the greatest problem with masturbation, but some married men struggle with this also, and some even as older men. Among women, masturbation is most common among singles, but some married women struggle as well, particularly when they have unsatisfactory relationships with their husbands.

For men, masturbation is usually motivated by sexual desire. A man who wants to live above masturbation then, needs to learn how to deal with sexual desire. For a woman, sexual desire may also be involved, but the deeper issue is usually relational. She wants closeness, understanding, and security; and masturbation is a way to calm the pain of relational emptiness. A man is vulnerable to the temptation to masturbate simply by a buildup of semen, as well as by sights, thoughts, or memories that stir sexual desire. A woman is vulnerable to the temptation to masturbate when she is lonely or unfulfilled in relationship. If she learns to use masturbation to dull her pain, eventually this may become the means to relieve other tensions as well.

These distinctions are not universal. Sometimes men also masturbate to relieve tension, and sometimes women have fed their sexual desires to where they are out of control—or in control. Understanding these basic differences between men and women, however, can help us find effective means of bringing sexual desires and activities under control.

3. Masturbation is not referred to specifically in the Bible.

The Bible speaks of lustful thoughts, evil desires, fornication, adultery, bestiality, flirting, and immodesty, but there is no direct reference to masturbation. Some readers of the KJV have thought Paul means masturbation in 1 Corinthians 6:9, when he refers to "abusers of themselves with mankind." But this is actually a reference to homosexual activities.

Although the Bible does not address masturbation specifically, it does give us direction. For, as we noted earlier, masturbation is an expression of sexual desire, and the Bible is abundant in guidelines for our sexual desires.

IS MASTURBATION A MORAL ISSUE?

Long ago, older people advised adolescents that masturbation was harmful to their health. The fear of deformities, of not developing into healthy adults, even of losing mental capacities, kept many young people from masturbation. Although this misinformation was widely believed, the warnings simply were not true. There is no known physical or mental damage caused by masturbation.

Even so, I believe masturbation is wrong, for a number of reasons:

1. *Masturbation engages sexuality contrary to God's design.* God designed us as sexual beings. His Word clearly teaches that sex is the expression of marital love (see Song of Solomon 4 and Proverbs 5:15-21). Masturbation takes sex out of its context of love in the lifelong commitment of marriage.

2. *Masturbation doesn't give and doesn't share, but is focused on self.* God designed that a man be sexually aroused by a woman (and woman by man) in the context of love in marriage. Masturbation is sexually arousing oneself. It is taking without giving. The person masturbating does not move outside of himself, only into himself. No one is enriched, spoken to, ministered to, loved, or cared for. It is self pleasing self.

3. *Masturbation leaves a person feeling empty.* We know

from the teaching of the Bible and from observation, that people who live for themselves are not happy or fulfilled. They are empty. Masturbation is empty because it is self-focused. But even more, the emptiness is amplified because sex was designed to be interactive. If a person spends all his money on himself, his life will be empty. But masturbation is worse than spending money on oneself. It is like trying to play softball by oneself—trying to be a team all by oneself and filling in the opposing team with imaginary characters. Imagine a person pitching the ball, hitting the ball, chasing the ball, throwing the ball, running the bases, making a tag—all by himself. It would be a lonely and discouraging ball game. Because sex was designed to be interactive, masturbation is empty and unfulfilling.

4. *Masturbation doesn't satisfy sexual hunger but feeds it.* A person who masturbates can experience a physical thrill and a sexual release, but he cannot experience sexual union or the joy of mutual love. The one-sided, self-focused experience only amplifies the reality that this is not true sexual pleasure; it is an imagination of it. Because masturbation leaves the heart dissatisfied with what it has just experienced, it also makes the heart hungrier for what it has not experienced.

5. *Masturbation is virtually impossible to do without lustful thoughts.* That is, it stirs in us a desire for what is not ours to have. A man typically visualizes images in his mind of a woman (or uses pictures of a woman to stir his desires). Or a man (or a woman) may try in an imaginary way to act out a scene in a story or carry forward a scene he experienced in interaction with a woman. In any case, the person in one's imagination is not one's

legitimate marriage partner. Jesus said, "Whosoever looketh on a woman to lust after her hath committed adultery with her already in his heart" (Matthew 5:28). (Note: Some children discover the pleasure of masturbation as a non-sexual activity. But as they develop sexually, it is normal for masturbation to become a sexual activity for them; that is, they learn that interactions with, and fantasies about, the opposite gender are integral to the activity.)

6. *Masturbation puts a person in an unreal world and sets him up for unreal expectations.* One of the damaging effects of masturbation is that one progressively builds a way of thinking and acting sexually outside actual, loving interaction with a real partner. When a person develops the habit of masturbation, the imaginary world of sexual activity is not only self-centered, but it is also unreal. One's sexual partner moves, talks, and responds (in the mind's eye) at the beck and call of one's own sexual desires. This can set up expectations that a real marriage partner finds virtually impossible to fulfill.

7. *Masturbation leaves a person feeling dirty and cheap.* As we have noted, masturbation takes something intended for an expression of marital love and turns it into a self-focused activity. It is a departure from the inherent intention of sex. As such, it carries an inherent shame. A husband and wife having sexual relations would want that activity to be private, but they would not be ashamed of what they are doing as long as it is made noble by thoughtfulness, tenderness, commitment, and self-discipline. A person who masturbates, however, is exercising none of those qualities. He has none of the hard work of building a relationship, of sac-

rifice, of keeping himself for another, or of cultivating faithfulness. Sex, for him, is not the priceless reward of a relationship well-built. It is available in any darkened corner. For the person who masturbates, sex is cheap. And cheap sex is shameful. I have seen the agonized look of those snared by masturbation—the shame of needing to talk about it can be difficult, but it is not as severe as the agonizing and lonely shame of continuing in bondage.

8. *Masturbation eats away at true manhood and womanhood.* It does not build respect for oneself. The man or woman who masturbates is not cultivating the qualities that make up true manhood and womanhood. No woman looks up to a man who masturbates regularly and admires him for his character, and vice versa. We are repelled by selfishness. And it seems the selfishness that finds expression in sex (whether by words, humor, actions, or body language) is particularly revolting, especially as it shapes the person over years. The man who spends his life in selfish pursuit of sexual pleasure becomes less and less admirable to women. And the woman who spends her life flirting, lusting, and stimulating her body becomes less and less attractive as a woman. Sexual selfishness (including masturbation, but not limited to it) undermines true manhood and womanhood.

And so I believe masturbation is wrong. It is selfish in nature, contrary to God's design for our sexuality, and like all sin, makes the sinner a miserable slave. I do not believe that masturbation is the worst of sins (although to a person enslaved to masturbation, it can appear so). But I believe when we view it as sinful, we can apply Biblical principles for living in victory over it. And there is deliverance!

The following help is given to those who see masturbation as wrong and are serious about learning to control their sexual desires.

HOW CAN A PERSON BREAK THE HABIT OF MASTURBATION?

The answers to this question are several. Their application, of course, can vary with individuals, but they are common to all sin. We will start with a number of basic principles and then look at a list of practical pointers.

1. We need to want deliverance.

Although human will alone is not enough to break the power of sexual sin, we will not find deliverance until we really do want it. As the Apostle Paul indicated, we can have conflicting forces within us. "For I know that in me (that is, in my flesh,) dwelleth no good thing: for to will is present with me; but how to perform that which is good I find not. For the good that I would I do not: but the evil which I would not, that I do" (Romans 7:18, 19).

If we are honest, we must admit that sometimes we don't want to be free from sexual sin. We like it. It makes us feel guilty, so we don't want it to be in control of our lives. But we don't want it to go far away. And we are secretly happy to see it return.

Freedom from sexual sin calls for more than a one-time choice. It calls for aligning our wills with the holy will of God. "For this is the will of God, even your sanctification, that ye should abstain from fornication: that every one of you should know how to possess his vessel in sanctification and honour" (1 Thessalonians 4:3, 4). The one who would be delivered must establish in his heart—I am fully committed to live a morally pure life, to conduct my body in a way that is holy.

2. We need to confess our sin before God so we can experience heart cleansing.

"If we confess our sins," the Apostle John assures us, "he is faithful and just to forgive us our sins, and to cleanse us from all unrighteousness" (1 John 1:9). To confess means simply to say what is true. Although confession for cleansing is an elementary spiritual law, we sometimes overlook its significance. We make hasty, general confessions and expect instant, total cleansing.

For a person wanting freedom from masturbation, it is essential to work from a clean heart. This is more than saying, "God, I did it again. I'm sorry."

CLEANSING THE HEART.

If you have never done a thorough heart cleansing of immoral involvements, here is a guide. Look at the following list of ways people violate pure living and mark (or list on another sheet of paper) those you are guilty of:

1. _____ Purposely gazing at sexual features (especially in certain positions or when the opposite sex is scantily clothed).
2. _____ Fantasizing about a particular woman/man.
3. _____ Reading sexually explicit stories.
4. _____ Watching sexually explicit or sexually suggestive videos or shows.

5. _____ Looking at pictures, magazines, or advertising media that show undress.

6. _____ Perusing medical media, dictionaries, or encyclopedias for sexual stimulation.

7. _____ Visually invading the privacy of the opposite sex (such as David watching Bathsheba bathe).

8. _____ Touching the opposite sex, bumping or brushing against bodies.

9. _____ Arranging secret meetings.

10. _____ Sending secret messages (via notes or electronic media).

11. _____ Using suggestive language, telling off-color jokes.

12. _____ Dressing/appearing in ways that attract attention to one's physical features.

13. _____ Exposing one's self to others.

14. _____ Going to topless bars, nude bars, or other places of "adult entertainment."

15. _____ Buying sensual "toys."

16. _____ Posting sensual messages, pictures, or jokes for others to see.

17. _____ Flirting (winking, waving, seeking the attention of the opposite sex).

18. _____ Teasing others in sensual or suggestive ways.

19. _____ Encouraging others to engage in sexual activities.

20. _____ Playing with clothing of the opposite sex.

21. _____ Cross-dressing.

22. _____ Sharing personal items (lip care, coffee cups, etc.) for arousal.

23. _____ Sharing personal information, especially of a sensual nature, to arouse another or to be aroused.

24. _____ Sexually stimulating oneself.
25. _____ Using animals for sexual pleasure or sexually stimulating animals.
26. _____ Fornication/adultery.
27. _____ Partner swapping.
28. _____ Introducing children to sexual activities.
29. _____ Incest (sexual activities with family members).
30. _____ Homosexual or lesbian activities (sensual touching, kissing, or having sexual relations with someone of the same sex).
31. _____ Offering to do sexual favors for hire.
32. _____ Paying for sexual favors.
33. _____ Cybersex or phone sex.
34. _____ Mentally reliving encounters with the opposite sex.
35. _____ Other: _____ .

When you have identified your sins specifically, take the list before the Lord, and say what is true (confess honestly) to Him. Although you can do this alone, you may find it helpful to do this with someone who can be your spiritual mentor. Ask God for a thorough cleansing of your heart, and express your desire to turn from these sins to a life that honors His will for your body. Some people find it helpful to write out their prayer to God, as David did in Psalm 51.

BLESSINGS OF CONFESSION.

The value of this kind of confession is twofold. First, by thorough confession, you are giving sin no cover under which to hide. As we discussed in Chapter 7, you are "walking in the light." One of the dangers of sexual sin is that because it is extremely pleasurable, our "flesh" would like to give it some place of hiding. Without being honest with ourselves, we are cherishing secret sin, still wanting to have it in some way, even while the spiritual part of us wants victory over sexual sin. The psalmist says, "If I regard iniquity in my heart [secretly cherish it], the Lord will not hear me" (Psalm 66:18). Thorough confession exposes those hidden areas that keep us from being honest with God.

The second blessing of thorough confession is the refreshing liberty of a clean heart. We do not realize how heavy sin is (even "little" secret sins) until we are cleansed through the blood of Jesus. Thorough confession exposes the filth of the flesh to the light of God, and God's immediate response is to apply the cleansing blood of Jesus. The experience of thorough cleansing is spiritually liberating—there is relief from burdens we didn't even know we were carrying, freedom to look others in the eye, and overwhelming joy in responding to the One who forgives.

This "clean heart" (spoken of by David in Psalm 51) is a treasure we want to retain. The freedom of a truly cleansed heart gives us a resolve not to return to sin. It acts as a powerful incentive to keep walking in righteousness.

3. We need to properly fill the empty areas in our lives.

Jesus said, "When the unclean spirit is gone out of a man, he walketh through dry places, seeking rest, and findeth none. Then he saith, I will return into my house from whence I came out; and when he is come, he findeth it empty, swept, and garnished. Then goeth he, and taketh with himself seven other spirits more wicked than himself, and they enter in and dwell there: and the last state of that man is worse than the first" (Matthew 12:43-45).

This teaching of Jesus reflects several things about the human heart. It is restless when empty; and in that empty restlessness, it is vulnerable to being filled wrongly. The heart emptied of evil must be filled with something better, or the person easily turns from one evil to another and is worse off than before.

God's intent in ridding the heart of sin always extends beyond forgiveness and cleansing. He is interested in more even than better behavior in the cleansed person's life. God wants to live in the cleansed heart. He wants to take up permanent residence. This was discussed at length in Chapter 7 ("put ye on the Lord Jesus Christ"), but as it relates to masturbation, there are still a number of points we need to consider.

Masturbation and its accompanying activities (such as fantasizing and looking at pornography) can be addictive. These sins are powerful in their binding effect. They call the person back into sin over and over, even after consequences have set in and the person clearly understands that he is destroying such precious things as his marriage, his family, his testimony, his spiritual ministry, and his own soul. The person gets so hooked that in Biblical terminology, his eyes are "full of adultery" and he "cannot cease from sin" (2 Peter 2:14).

With all addictions, we must understand an important principle: addictions develop out of, and are sustained by, emptiness. While this seems especially true for ladies who struggle with masturbation, it applies to men as well. So before we consider that God wants to take up residence in our hearts, we do well to let Him search out the true condition of our hearts. In so doing, we will typically find empty areas—places

of hidden longing, deep disappointment, crushed relationships, or unmet needs.

These empty areas provide a hotbed for desires. We want
approval, acceptance, recognition, or love. We want to be
noticed. Sometimes we yearn and simply don't know what we
want. "Hope deferred," the proverb goes, "maketh the heart
sick, but when the desire cometh, it is a tree of life" (Proverbs
13:12). We don't do well and we don't grow well when strongly
held expectations are not fulfilled. In the "hotbed" analogy,
even legitimate desires may grow fast and furiously. But like
plants left too long in the hotbed, they become spindly and
dangerously overgrown, and eventually topple in ruin.

Tragically a life driven by unmet longings often turns to
the wrong things for satisfaction. People turn to money, fame,
pleasure, possessions, and sensual indulgence to fill the void
inside. If our culture is indeed an empty culture, it is no wonder people are "hooked" on everything imaginable.

The good news is that God is fully able to meet us at exactly
the area of our deepest emptiness. Thus, He can be a father
to the fatherless, a husband to the widow, a friend to the forsaken, a healer to the wounded, water to the thirsty, food to
the hungry, an identity to the nobodies, a shepherd to the
lost, a protector to those who have no defense, a rock to those
whose world is in upheaval. God is incredibly able and willing to meet humans exactly where they are.

But we must remember, He is *much more* than a God who
understands and responds to human needs. Over and over in
Scriptural accounts, we have God meeting human beings at
the exact place of their extreme need.

In addressing the habit of masturbation, then, especially
one that is deeply entrenched, we must look squarely and
discerningly at the underlying emptiness. For ladies, this

emptiness is often lurking around the hunger for relationship; for men, it is often centered on a yearning for acceptance or recognition. Sometimes these hungers reflect legitimate and understandable yearnings (as when a person has grown up with abuse or continual disapproval from parents), and other times they simply reflect our selfishness and pride (we fear rejection, for example, and set out to find approval in the wrong ways from the wrong people).

Here are a number of ways emptiness can develop:

1. We have experienced rejection in a meaningful friendship.
2. We have had deep disappointment in our relationship with our parents.
3. We have grown up with physical abuse.
4. A parent was notorious for something shameful (drunkenness, immorality, poor management, etc.).
5. We have been teased, ridiculed, or rejected by family or peers.
6. We have feared rejection because our family is markedly distinct from families around us (for example, our family is poor or follows ultra-strict guidelines that set us apart from others).
7. We have a physical deformity or handicap that makes us different from others or that keeps us from enjoying what others experience (such as walking, seeing, or getting married).
8. We think we are ugly (or we fear we are). In a culture that emphasizes physical attractiveness, even physically attractive people often fear they are not.
9. We have grown up with an emphasis on strict behavior or performance so that we regularly feel guilty. This may be in one's home or church setting.

Looking at a list such as this, we must beware of several dangers. The first is the danger of blaming our problems on others. Although it is true that emptiness is the context in which driving desires develop, we are wrong to view our emptiness as the sole cause for our problems and our sins, and thus blame whoever was most responsible for our emptiness. This is an age-old human tendency. We don't want to take responsibility for our own actions.

If we study the emptiness in our lives in order to find someone to blame—or if in finding who is responsible for our emptiness, we begin blaming them—we will quickly open ourselves to a host of both personal and interpersonal problems. This approach has unfortunately been promoted by popular psychology and has been picked up and supported by many Christian counselors as well. Parents get the blame today for virtually everything wrong with their children. (And, of course, we must avoid reacting to this unhealthy blame mentality and thereby deny that parents have anything to do with the problems of their children.)

The reality is that parents do neglect, abuse, and damage their children. This is not new, although conditions in our day are exacerbating the problem. Too many children have empty hearts and then turn to vandalism, drugs, pleasure, and sensual sins to fill their emptiness. Parents must accept responsibility for their neglect, and children must accept responsibility for their wrong reactions.

The point is that if we face the emptiness in our lives to find who is to blame for it, we will stumble. By focusing on "their" responsibility (no matter who "they" are), we can miss the truth of our own responsibility and the opportunity we have to find the fullness of God at the very place of our emptiness, and, in Christ, to choose new and better responses to those who have hurt or disappointed us. Some people never recover from the discovery of who is to blame for their emptiness. By holding others responsible, they further ruin their relationship with parents, family members, former friends, their church, or its leaders.

The second danger in facing the emptiness that may drive such problems as masturbation is assuming that understanding the problem resolves it. This tendency is again reflected in both modern psychology and much Christian counseling. We seem driven to explain wrong behavior, its causes and its symptoms, with the underlying assumption that understanding what is wrong will in itself correct what is wrong. This unfortunate assumption serves actually to protect many psychologists and counselors from the inefficiency of their counseling. By offering complicated, and sometimes even accurate, descriptions of our problems, they project the notion that explanation is the answer. The person struggling with the problem is distracted from the desire to change by focusing instead on explaining what is wrong. The result is again a way out of accepting personal responsibility.

Onlookers are seldom impressed. They hear the explanation, and in their minds say, "Yes, well, but you still are no better off than you were." Only the person with the problem (and the complicated explanation) seems unaware of what he is actually doing.

The irony of explaining to avoid doing has been the subject of many jokes. One man, for example, went to his psychiatrist and said, "Doctor, tell me in plain words what is wrong with me."

The doctor looked at him and said, "Your problem is that you are lazy."

"Oh," the man replied. "Now tell me in medical terms, so

I can go home and tell my wife."

The goal of facing our emptiness is not so we can blame others, not so we can explain our wrong behavior, but so we can rightly turn to God.

Every human problem has its roots somehow in our departure from God, and every solution to our problem must have its roots in our return to God. If we are plagued with an enslaving habit of masturbation, we do well to take the time to identify the emptiness in which our sexual desire grew to such unhealthy proportions. There we may find a huge yearning for acceptance, recognition, closeness, etc. We can take our wrong responses to God in repentance—not repentance here for the resultant sins (such as masturbation) but for using wrong means to satisfy our desires.

By not turning to God first, we have "committed two evils" as God said of His people many years ago. "They have forsaken me the fountain of living waters, and hewed them out cisterns, broken cisterns, that can hold no water" (Jeremiah 2:13).

God stands ready to fill the empty lives of those who have turned to wrong fountains to satisfy the desires of their hearts. Masturbation can temporarily relieve the pain of rejection, the cry of a lonely heart, the resentment for abuse, the bitterness of one who can never marry. But it can never fill the heart with peace. Those who turn to sexual pleasure to relieve inner tensions are carving out a cistern that is broken from the start. It holds no water. It leaves the heart continually emptier, thirstier, and less satisfied.

God calls us to bring our emptiness to Him. "Ho, every one that thirsteth," He calls. "Come ye to the waters, and he that hath no money; come ye, buy, and eat; yea, come, buy wine and milk without money and without price. Wherefore do ye spend money for that which is not bread? and your labour for that which satisfieth not? hearken diligently unto me, and eat ye that which is good, and let your soul delight itself in fatness" (Isaiah 55:1, 2).

DEALING WITH EMPTINESS.

1. Look at the list of ways emptiness develops. For each one, name the desire(s) that could grow into a driving force under those conditions (desire for acceptance, recognition, etc.)

2. If you see that you have been driven by emptiness, describe as accurately as possible the conditions in which your emptiness developed.

3. Name the desire or desires you have had as a result of those conditions.

4. Describe honestly how those desires have shaped your attitudes.

5. Describe how those desires have driven your behavior.

6. Take some time to pray and consider how God is able to meet your desire. This may take some time. You should consider any Scriptural examples of people who have faced situations similar to yours—what can you learn from them? How did they find (or miss) God in their distress? You may also look up verses that speak to the particular desire that has driven you. Study these Scriptural examples and texts until you have gained a clear picture of God's ability to meet you at the place of your need.

7. Begin a journal or a record of what you learn in your journey with God. You may record your struggles as well as your blessings. Begin a list of verses that

describe God in ways that are especially meaningful to you.

8. As you continue this study, you will want to list healthy, God-honoring ways of responding to the particular conditions (and people) in which your emptiness developed. That is, as you see your unhealthy responses (resentment, rage, despair, blame, self-pity, sensual indulgence, overeating, masturbation, etc.), you can ask God to show you what are healthy, right responses to these situations and people. How does He want you to view these things? How does He want you to respond? This list of responses is most meaningful as it grows out of your understanding of, and acquaintance with, God Himself. That is, although God cares about our behavior, He cares more that we learn to know Him. He is not as concerned that we stop masturbating as He is that we are attempting to find satisfaction apart from Him. Our acquaintance with His fullness, in other words, needs to be the base upon which we break our sinful habits.

9. Review the guidance in Chapter 7 for setting up safeguards. Although the presence of God is our greatest fortification against such sins as masturbation, we do well to set up safeguards that keep us from the places or situations in which we can be tempted.

10. All these steps are typically enhanced with the involvement of a meaningful friend or mentor.

A FEW PRACTICAL POINTERS.

Since masturbation is a highly sensual problem, we must pay careful attention to sensual stimulants. The eyes and ears and tactile senses are the senses most attuned to sexual stimulation. When we have been slaves to sexual activities, it takes effort and discipline to retrain the body in righteousness, bringing the senses back under the control of God's Holy Spirit.

Here are some practical pointers:

1. Take quick, moderately warm showers rather than long, hot baths.
2. Eat moderately and avoid high caloric foods, especially if your normal activities don't burn off a lot of calories. Keeping your eating habits in check is a helpful discipline in gaining control of sexual desires.
3. Read something spiritually enriching before going to bed.
4. As you wait for sleep to come, pray and meditate on what God has done for you that day.
5. When you wake up in the morning, get out of bed immediately rather than lazing for a time in half-sleep.
6. Place helpful mottoes or posters in strategic places (bathroom, bedroom, vehicle, work station, etc.).
7. When a particular person stirs you to sexual thoughts, begin to pray immediately for this person's spiritual welfare.
8. Form a link between sexual temptation and one particular need, such as a mission outreach, a missionary, or the spiritual needs of a person you know. This is better than praying specifically for victory over sexual temptation, for such a prayer keeps sexual temptation in focus; whereas prayer for someone else takes your thoughts down other paths. Consciously establish this link—as soon as you are tempted, switch to

intercession for that specific need. You can change the prayer need after a week or two, but keep the link in place.

9. Keep someone informed of your moral intentions and your progress. Meet regularly with this person to report and to pray together.

10. One man told me he needed to resort to more drastic measures to avoid masturbation. He committed himself to his pastor that if he failed, he would give $1,000 to the church offering. "I needed to have something that would hit me where it hurt," he said. At the time he reported this to me, he had been living in victory for some time! This is an application of the instruction of Jesus regarding sexual temptation, "Whosoever looketh on a woman to lust after her hath committed adultery with her already in his heart. And if thy right eye offend thee, pluck it out, and cast it from thee: for it is profitable for thee that one of thy members should perish, and not that thy whole body should be cast into hell" (Matthew 5:28, 29).

These pointers, of course, cannot in themselves break the habit of masturbation. They are intended to assist those who are walking daily with the Father and His Son, Jesus Christ. As Paul said, "Put ye on the Lord Jesus Christ, and make not provision for the flesh, to fulfil the lusts thereof" (Romans 13:14).

APPENDIX B:

HOMOSEXUALITY

"Because of this, God gave them
over to shameful lusts.
Even their women exchanged
natural relations for unnatural ones.
In the same way the men also
abandoned natural relations with women
and were inflamed with lust for one another.
Men committed indecent acts with other men,
and received in themselves the
due penalty for their perversion."
Romans 1:26, 27, NIV[1]

In our culture, homosexuality is an explosive topic. Longer ago, homosexuality was considered, even by non-Christians, to be abnormal and wrong. In today's ideological climate, any view other than acceptance can be labeled as rising from either hate or fear. Christians who say homosexual behavior is wrong are referred to as "homophobic" or as promoting "hate propaganda."

And so, we need to look at this subject wisely and honestly.

We must approach it with neither fear nor hatred for a number of reasons. First, because the call of the Gospel reaches to everyone. That includes homosexuals. When they respond to the Gospel, we need to know how Jesus would have us relate to them. The second reason we need to look at this subject is because the issue of homosexuality is not just "out there." Some people who have grown up in Christian homes, and attended Christian schools and Christian churches are, nonetheless, attracted to members of the same sex. These people need our understanding and our help.

We must avoid making judgments based on either ignorance or misinformation. And we must have the courage to face the issues honestly, lovingly, and Biblically.

I would like to start with a number of observations from the Bible (particularly from the passage quoted at the beginning of this appendix). We will look then at a number of facts about homosexuality, and conclude with helpful principles for addressing homosexuality.

SOME OBSERVATIONS FROM THE BIBLE.

1. Homosexuality increases under certain cultural conditions.

The first chapter of Romans charts the downward spiral of a culture that departs from God. The denial of God leads almost inevitably to the elevation of man. As man becomes great in his own eyes, he makes "discoveries" that further his delusions. The pursuit of knowledge in the context of denying God is almost intoxicating—man professes himself to be wise while staggering about in foolishness.

In such a setting, sin multiplies, especially sexual sin. Man becomes more like an animal—actually, cut loose from moral restraints, he becomes worse than the animals. In a godless, humanistic, sinful society, he gives free rein to his sexual desires, and all sorts of sexual sins march boldly out of the closet. Homosexual behavior is only one of many.

Thus, in Sodom, as sin abounded, so also did homosexuality. The same thing happened in Israel centuries later (see Judges 19).

The other side of this truth is that homosexuality is less frequent in groups that honor God, hold high moral standards, and cultivate strong family interaction.

2. Homosexuality is a departure from what is natural.

Paul refers to homosexual behavior as "against nature," causing people to do "unseemly" or "indecent" acts. Until 1973 the American Psychiatric Association listed homosexuality as a disorder, but today psychiatrists and psychologists rarely see it so. Consequently, many people today believe homosexuals are "just born that way" or have a homosexual orientation.

The Bible teaches us that God planned for male and female to be attracted to each other, and that sexual attraction to the same sex is a perversion of God's plan. If a person's "orientation" is toward members of the same sex, we see this as a disorientation, as a disorder. And homosexual behavior, then, is abnormal behavior.

With this view, we do not deny that some people are attracted to members of the same sex or that people can develop a same-sex orientation, but we believe they have been "twisted" in development. We do not believe homosexuality is an orientation a person is born with, but a disorientation a person develops in the formative stages of life. Although the factors involved in the "twisting" can be complicated (and we must avoid assuming one malformation fits all), the more important issue is that it is a formative problem, not a genetic problem.

The formative understanding of homosexuality offers hope, for if a person can be wrongly formed, he or she can also be re-formed. That is, a person whose sexual desires have become homosexual can be redirected to become heterosexual, as thousands of changed people can testify. Joe Dallas, himself a former homosexual, writes, "People tend to view homosexuality more favorably when they think it is inborn. No wonder gay leaders (not all, but most) push the born gay theory; it furthers the cause."[2] Dr. Joseph Nicolosi states emphatically, "We are all heterosexual. Some heterosexuals have a homosexual problem, but it does not mean there are two different kinds of people."[3] And Stanton Jones, who is the Chair of Psychology at Wheaton College, writes, "Anyone who says there is no hope (for change) is either ignorant or a liar. Every secular study of change has shown some success rate, and persons who testify to substantial healings by God are legion."[4]

3. Homosexuality is even more shameful than other sexual sins.

In Chapter 2, we noted that sexual sins carry a distinct shame. The shame of adultery is greater than that of stealing, for example (as noted in Proverbs 6:30-33). For this reason, in a culture of increased sin and a subsequent decrease in shame about sexual sins, homosexual sins "come out" with increased frequency and boldness.

What many today hail as "progress," then, is actually regression. The story in Judges 19-21 vividly shows us the shame of homosexual sins and what happens when a culture takes that path. The whole nation of Israel was sliding into sexual promiscuity. In that new "freedom," some young men of Benjamin boldly demanded to have sex (same-sex) with a Levite stopping for the night in Gibeah.

Their sexual abuse of the Levite's servant wife killed her. What raised the wrath of the other tribes, however, does not seem to be the horrible abuse of the lady so much as the shameful desires of the men. The nation was shocked. This was almost identical to the sin of the Sodomites against Lot's visitors! Their united message to the tribe of Benjamin was, "What wickedness is this that is done among you? Now therefore deliver us the men, the children of Belial, which are in Gibeah, that we may put them to death, and put away evil from Israel" (Judges 20:12, 13).

In saying that sexual sins are more shameful than stealing or lying, and that some sexual sins (such as homosexuality and pedophilia) are more shameful than other sexual sins, we are not saying that these sins are more sinful. We are simply recognizing the progression of sexual sins and the resultant shame.

4. Because homosexuality is a perversion of sexuality, it is easy to react wrongly to homosexuals.

This reflects a universal human problem. The Bible says we are all sinners, barring none. And yet we easily categorize sins and look down our noses at those with "worse" sins than ours. In such a frame of mind, we can be arrogant, judgmental, harsh, critical, scornful, and shamefully hurtful. (Consider the account of the adulterous woman and her accusers in John 8.)

In the story of the homosexuals in Gibeah, we see the harsh responses of the Israelites. Although the sin of the young men was great and did call for punishment, the ensuing tragedies show that God was not pleased with the attitude of the eleven tribes either. In the heat of their indignation, the Israelites not only set out to bring the offenders to justice, but they made a vow not to give their daughters in marriage to a Benjamite. How easy it is to make harsh judgments when looking at sins that seem worse than our own!

When they asked God if they should go to war against the tribe of Benjamin, He said yes. But instead of giving them victory, God allowed the Benjamites to destroy 22,000 men. The next day, God again said yes, and they lost 18,000 more men. On the third day, God gave the victory to the Israelites, and all but 600 men of the tribe of Benjamin were destroyed.

Why such tragic losses? We conclude that although the Israelites were right in condemning what the young men of Gibeah had done, they deserved the same judgment they were so eager to inflict. Sin is wrong. But all sin is wrong. Before we deal with sin in anyone else, we must be willing to judge our own lives by the same standards. In our indignation about sin in others, we may be pronouncing our own sentences, for the way we judge others is the way we shall be judged. Or as James says, "He shall have [receive] judgment without mercy, that hath shewed no mercy" (James 2:13).

Thus, in discussing the sin of homosexual behavior, we must beware of a number of potential sins ourselves. We must not have double standards. Heterosexual sins are no less sinful than homosexual sins. Furthermore, when we point out sin, we must be neither unkind nor judgmental of the persons involved. Before God, we all stand in need of mercy and forgiveness. In looking at sins of others, we must not do so with an attitude of superiority. We all have the same bent to evil.

5. When sexual sins are given legitimacy, they eventually are demanded as a right.

God designed sex to be the expression of love between a husband and wife in lifelong marriage. When sexual passions are given freedom to violate God's laws, they become the expressions of selfishness. A society that protects sexual sins, whether heterosexual or homosexual, will find perpetuators of those sins turning to violent means to demand their sexual privileges.

Thus, the men of Gibeah demanded sex with the Levite. When they could not have him, they sexually violated his servant wife until she died. The tendency to turn to violence for sex and to demand sex is very common in the West, especially among homosexuals. Homosexual rallies have easily turned violent, especially if anyone dares to offer a different viewpoint.

I witnessed this firsthand some years ago in New York City. I went with a group of Christians to Washington Park to distribute Christian literature and talk to people about Jesus. Unknown to us, a homosexual rally was planned for the same weekend in the same park. Not knowing what the bandstand and crowds were about, we left that area, moved to the other end of the park and began our work. In a short time, men began marching around our group, holding protest signs reading, "God is gay," etc. The police arrived and shortly advised us to leave the park, telling us, "We cannot secure your safety."

SOME FACTS ABOUT HOMOSEXUALITY.

Since this subject is so controversial and since beliefs on both (or many) sides are held so strongly, we have a hard time distinguishing between fact and fancy, between objective truth and subjective bias.

For years, the popular notion (based on a flawed study by "experts") was that ten percent of the population was homosexual. In spite of evidence to the contrary, many people quoted this statistic long after it was known to be inaccurate. Research in the early 1990s concluded that three to four percent of men and only one to two percent of women are homosexual.[5] Combining these figures, only about two percent of the population is homosexual.

But the same psychology text that reports these findings downplays environment as a factor in the development of a homosexual orientation. The writer says, "The bottom line from a half-century's theory and research: If there are environmental factors that influence sexual orientation, we do not know what they are."[6] And yet on the same page, the author reports that nine in ten children raised by lesbian couples developed into heterosexuals. (He states this positively, of course.) At that rate, one in ten of these children developed into homosexuals, which is a rate 500 to 1000 percent higher than the national norm of one to two percent. Still the author says naively, "Studies suggest that being reared by lesbian or gay parents does not appreciably affect a child's sexual orientation."[7] If one in ten as compared to one or two in a hundred is not an appreciable increase, we might wonder just what kind of increase would have to occur to be noticed by psychologists as an environmental factor!

Let's consider some facts:

1. Only about two percent of the adult population is homosexual.

2. Homosexual behavior does not always indicate homosexual orientation.

3. The Bible describes homosexual behavior as sinful.

4. The Bible describes homosexuality as a developmental problem that increases in the context of certain cultural conditions.

5. It is the willful involvement in homosexual activity that is sinful, not the disorientation itself.

6. A homosexual disorientation can be changed.

7. Reorientation is a process that takes time.

William Consiglio, in his book *Homosexual No More*, lists another fact about homosexuality (in a list of ten facts) that is worth considering. He says, "Homosexuality has very little to do with sex."[8] It has far more to do with unmet yearnings in former relationships. He quotes Dr. Elisabeth Moberly saying that the "homosexual impulse" is driven by "the need to make good earlier deficits in the parent-child relationship. The persistent need for love from the same sex stems from . . . the earlier unmet need for love from the parent of the same sex, or rather, the inability to receive such love, whether or not it was offered."[9] Notice the clarification that it is not always the parent's lack of love, but may also be, for various reasons, the child's inability (or difficulty) to receive that love.

HELP FOR THOSE WHO STRUGGLE WITH HOMOSEXUAL DESIRES.

In offering help, I want to note a number of things. Individual situations vary, and although we can look at principles that apply generally, every person will have individual issues that call for wise and careful understanding. Furthermore, homosexual orientation is highly personal. Facing it calls for courage. Enabling others to face it calls for love and understanding. Christians struggling with same-sex attractions are sometimes so ashamed of these attractions that they may live with them for years before confiding in someone else. Homosexuals who come to Christ after years of homosexual activity face similar struggles. Some who have attempted to face these issues have been further wounded by the attitudes, admonitions, and misguided efforts of fellow Christians.

We believe it is possible for homosexuals to change. We believe it is possible to recognize homosexual behavior as sinful and still deal compassionately and redemptively with sinners. We believe there are people who have homosexual desires who are not yielding to those desires and are committed Christians.

Let's turn to some guidance.

1. A person with homosexual desires should view those desires as wrong expressions of his or her sexuality.

This is a matter of viewpoint about these desires, not a matter of condemnation nor a call to self-loathing. It means simply that we must agree with God that homosexuality is "against nature" (Romans 1:26). Although homosexual desires may seem to be "just how I am," we must view them as "how I have become" rather than "how I was made." In other words, a person has a homosexual orientation as a result of wrong formation, rather than genetic construction.

This is the same view a person must have who struggles with any other sexual desires contrary to God's design. If a man is attracted sexually to children, he must view this as a wrong expression of his sexuality, not as something legitimate or normal just because he has those desires. Similarly, if a man has a sexual fixation on a certain kind of ladies' apparel, or a strong sexual attraction to a particular lady who is not his wife, he must view those desires as urging him to wrong expressions of his sexuality, not as legitimate.

2. A person with homosexual desires must be willing to face the issues involved in the formation of those desires.

This is probably the most painful and difficult part of the process of change. As with all "looking back" in one's life, the goal is to face issues as they are, not to blame other people, even when other people have not done right.

The three most common factors in the formation of same-sex desires are these: 1) Self-concepts. 2) Relationship with parents. 3) Relationships with peers. In general, this is also the order of significance for these three factors, although that varies with individuals.

Same-sex attractions are always linked to unhealthy or distorted self-concepts. Many people refer to this as a problem of "poor self-esteem." Although this is not totally wrong, it can also be misleading, for it promotes the idea that we must have a good opinion of ourselves, and that others (particularly parents, teachers, and preachers) must make their contribution to our good opinion of ourselves, or they fail their job. Countless adult problems have been hung on this theory.

The better understanding and terminology is that children sometimes develop an unhealthy and debilitating shame about themselves. There is a good sense of shame that kicks in when we do something stupid or sinful. This good shame is not always with us, but it stands ready to give us a red face when we make a huge blunder or do something we know we ought not to do. Healthy shame keeps us on our toes to avoid doing wrong, and it also motivates us to correct our mistakes, offer appropriate apologies, and make restitution to the best of our ability. Guided by healthy shame, we can be restored to good standing in our own conscience and in the minds of others.

Unhealthy shame, on the other hand, is shame about who we are, not so much about what we may have done. It is always with us, not just when we do wrong. Instead of standing ready to kick in at the appropriate time and motivating us to make things right, it regularly kicks us about, inhibiting healthy behavior and interaction. We live in dread of discovery, in continual shame, and often with a deep fear of rejection.

For some children, this is not only a matter of personal shame. It can also include a shame of family, shame of particular conditions, or shame about one's parent(s).

Not all children who grow up with shame, of course, become homosexual. A major part of personal identity is gender identity—a boy comes to identify himself with men and a girl identifies herself with women. It is when unhealthy shame about oneself is coupled with unhealthy development of gender identity that a child is in danger of developing same-sex attractions.

Although parents are the most powerful external communicators of gender identity, many other factors contribute to it. Cultural norms (what makes one a "real man" or a "real woman" in the minds of people), the significant people in one's extended family and church (aunts, uncles, grandparents, preachers, and teachers), cross-gender activities (who children play with as children and what kinds of activities they engage in), even children's toys can make their contribution to gender development and gender identity.

Negative factors in the development of gender identity include, but are not limited to, the following:

1) Emptiness in relationship with one's same-gender par-

ent; that is, failure to establish deep and meaningful relationship between father and son or between mother and daughter, or awkwardness or embarrassment or unmet desires in physical expressions of affection.

2) Deep shame about one's gender or one's sexuality (through sexual abuse or exploitation).

3) Strong negative feelings associated with an opposite-gender parent (such as a boy repulsed by his dominant mother).

4) Deep embarrassment about one's same-gender parent (as when a boy is teased or rejected because of his father).

5) Unhealthy relationship with one's peers in gender development—teasing about one's gender, for example.

6) Lack of gender affirmation—or worse, gender-specific criticism. (An example of gender affirmation would be, "You are strong, just like your dad." An example of gender-specific criticism would be, "You are a wimp, just like your dad.")

7) Unrealistic (or unhealthy) standards for behavior, set either by a poor parental model or by the child's own inner standards. Dr. Joseph Nicolosi, president of the National Association for Research and Treatment of Homosexuality, refers to this as a development of a "false self." The model behavior is artificial. He writes, "The false self is part of this good little boy. Such pre-homosexual boys are very polite, responsible, clean, neat, sensitive to other people, especially their mothers' needs, aware of what other people expect of them and tend to deny their own needs and wants and would rather make other people happy. . . . And that is why when men finally come out of the closet, they can

act up and become bad little boys. . . . Homosexual behavior is a way of being bad."[10]

These factors in themselves do not automatically produce same-sex attractions. When coupled with problems in personal development, however, or when in the mind of a child they come to be associated with gender identity, they can contribute to the formation of same-sex attractions.

Tracing the formation of one's self-concepts and gender identity is not always easy. It is difficult to be objective, and having a mature, caring mentor to guide a person through the process is essential.

3. A person willing to leave homosexuality must forsake his wrong responses to his development and pursue God's ways.

People recovered from homosexuality testify regularly to identifying such things in their lives as anger, rebellion, bitterness, hatred, shame, deep hurt, and desperate longings. Invariably, they come to see how they responded wrongly to parents, peers, abuse, or rejection. They had built walls, developed hardness of heart, made inner resolves, or pursued affirmation wrongly. Looking at these underlying issues showed them that their homosexual attractions were not so much sexual as they were reaching for such things as significance, affirmation, and love in wrong ways.

This calls for repentance—coming to God in sorrow for wrong choices and wrong turns in life and turning back to God's ways. Recovering from homosexuality involves such things as forgiving others, learning a proper sense of identity (rooted in belonging to God), distinguishing between healthy shame for wrongdoing and unhealthy shame about oneself, and learning how to love and trust other people in healthy ways.

It should not surprise us that since becoming a homosexual is a process (not simply a decision), recovering from homosexuality is likewise a process. We ought not to counsel a person simply to "choose to be different," as though that in itself will be enough. No one changes without right choices, but making a choice is not all that is necessary.

The process involves at least the following:

1) Accepting a right view of homosexuality. It is wrong. It is the result of wrong development, and therefore, it can be changed.
2) Identifying the specific factors that were involved in the wrong formation of one's own sexuality.
3) Reshaping one's sense of identity as a child of God and one's sexual identity according to God's design for one's gender.
4) Learning godly responses to those people or situations that were involved in wrong formation.

Change comes about in the right setting. Mike Haley, who practiced homosexual behavior from adolescence into adulthood, testifies to the power of a friend who never gave up on him. He describes his journey as one that began with this friend's faithful commitment to him, led him to a personal relationship with Jesus, and then found full restoration in the context of a caring, healthy church. Today, Mike has given his life to ministering to homosexuals who are seeking to be restored.[11]

Since recovery from homosexuality is a spiritual journey, it involves the church. God's people are naive to think that if a person is "saved" he will not need help with such issues. Several things are important in a church that is willing to disciple people from homosexuality to recovery.

1) We need to be truly Christo-centric. Having a person

conform to external standards of appearance or behavior will not be sufficient to meet the needs of his heart. We must lead people to true and meaningful relationship with Jesus.

2) We need to love people and demonstrate that love in caring, committed relationships in the church. Discipleship doesn't go well in a group that is self-righteous, critical, superficial, conceited, or full of gossip. On the other hand, the ability to love sinners is at the heart of godliness, for "God so loved the world, that he gave his only begotten Son" (John 3:16). And Jesus said, "By this shall all men know that ye are my disciples, if ye have love one to another" (John 13:35). If we have unholy, hateful, or cold attitudes among ourselves or toward sinners, we will never effectively minister to homosexuals.

3) We need to practice true holiness of life—demonstrating social purity, honesty, fairness in business deals, neighborly love, consideration for the poor, faithfulness in marriage, etc. Love for sinners does not mean compromise with sin. The church that would minister to homosexuals must stand against sin—not just the sin of homosexuality, but all sin.

4) We need to develop relationships at a level that is real and meaningful. That is, it must be safe not only for homosexuals to open up their lives in honesty, but for all members to be real with one another—where honesty is the prevailing way of life for members. A church that regularly projects where members ought to be, but rarely allows members to discuss where they are, simply is not a place where Christian discipleship will take place in meaningful ways.

SUMMARY

Homosexuality is a perversion of healthy sexuality. Because it is developed, there is also hope for change. Recovery from homosexuality, like its development, is a process. It is a spiritual process, calling for God's help in searching the heart and returning to His design. The process requires honesty. It can be painful and extended, and it typically calls for involvement from loving, caring friends. But recovery from homosexuality is a real possibility, and it is well worth the effort, as thousands of recovered homosexuals will readily testify.

HELPFUL RESOURCES:

Carlson, Jodi, (compiler), *The Truth Comes Out: The Roots and Causes of Male Homosexuality*, (Colorado Springs, 2001, a publication of Focus on the Family).

Carlson, Jodi, *The Heart of the Matter: The Roots and Causes of Female Homosexuality*, (Colorado Springs, 1999, a publication of Focus on the Family).

Consiglio, William, *Homosexual No More*. (Victor Books, 1991).

Haley, Mike, *Straight Answers: Exposing the Myths and Facts About Homosexuality*, (Colorado Springs, 2001, a publication of Focus on the Family).

APPENDIX C

RESTORING PURITY IN WOMEN

*And I will restore to you the years that the locust hath eaten,
the cankerworm, and the caterpillar, and the palmerworm,
my great army which I sent among you.
And ye shall eat in plenty, and be satisfied,
and praise the name of the LORD your God,
that hath dealt wondrously with you:
and my people shall never be ashamed.*
Joel 2:25, 26

After Tamar was raped by her brother, she tore her clothes, put ashes on her head, and "went on crying." The sad story concludes with this hauntingly brief narrative: "So Tamar remained desolate in her brother Absalom's house" (2 Samuel 13:20). Desolation—what a sad state in which to sort out the terrible shame and sorrow of sexual sin! Although it is the experience of many, it does not need to be so. In this appendix, we will explore how ladies who have been ensnared in sexual sin can be restored to purity.

Whether we are male or female, when we have sinned sexually, we need to repent (Chapter 4) and rebuild moral character (Chapter 5). There are a couple of issues for ladies, however, that call for a few additional thoughts:

1. Sexual sin reflects desperation for relationship.
2. Sexual sin is devastating to a woman's sense of femininity.

A woman who wishes to restore purity must understand these dimensions and respond wisely to be fully restored. Concerning the first issue, if she does not understand her yearning for relationship as a root issue, she may on the one hand try to squelch a vital part of herself as a woman or on the other hand open herself unwisely in future relationships with men. Concerning the second issue, if she does not regain a healthy sense of womanhood, she may allow her "ruined" view of herself to muddy her motivations in virtually all she does and dull her ability to make wise choices.

So let's further consider these two issues.

THE YEARNING FOR RELATIONSHIP.

When a woman gives her body to a man in an illicit affair, typically she is not driven by sexual desire so much as relational hunger. She wants a companion, a man who will cherish her, protect her, and provide for her. This yearning is ingrained in a woman.

When a girl grows up emotionally disconnected, especially disconnected from significant males in her family structure, the yearning for a man to know her and love her becomes a passion. She is not always honest with this yearning, and many times is unconscious of the way it drives her. But if she has no men of strength in her life who are involved enough to know her, respect her, and provide leadership for her, she is insecure and can be driven to fill the void in wrong ways.

This is the underlying yearning that causes a woman to ignore her moral standards and give her body to a man. She is seeking to satisfy this longing deep within her. It is so strong she may ignore pain, shame, rebuke, and advice to get it.

She is deluded, of course, and in her delusion she will have expectations for the man she's with that he knows nothing about. He is delighted by the pleasure she gives him, and typically he is driven by sexual desire with little intention of really developing a deep relationship (or clueless about what that means). To him, a deep relationship is what they do together. Inevitably her expectations and his cluelessness eventually collide. And she is left devastated.

TO RESTORE PURITY, A WOMAN MUST BUILD HEALTHY RELATIONSHIPS.

It is virtually impossible for a woman to leave sexual sin without dealing with the yearning to belong. This is not always possible. Sometimes a father is unwilling to become involved in ways that provide the security his daughter so desperately wants. Sometimes they have developed such poor habits of relating that they find it painfully slow going to build a meaningful relationship, and they give up in discouragement.

A woman committed to restoring purity must understand her yearning and commit herself to building right relationships. This involves both God and His people. One way to approach this is with resolves:

1. *I will begin a lifelong pursuit of communion with God.*

That is, I will look for the ways to cultivate my relationship with Him—reading books that help me toward God, developing meaningful devotional time, praying, and journaling—writing out my thoughts to God and chronicling my progress.

2. *I will pursue meaningful relationships with godly ladies.* That is, I will cultivate relationships with ladies who are spiritually mature, learning from them, observing the ways they handle their feelings, their bodies, and their unmet needs.

3. *I will place my yearning for a man in God's hands.* That is, I will refuse to try to make a relationship happen. I will accept a relationship only if I'm convinced God has arranged it and is giving it to me—and has confirmed it by the blessing of my parents and/or pastor.

4. *I will cultivate healthy relationships with male authority figures.* That is, to the extent I am able, I will build my relationship with my earthly father. This will mean forgiving him, removing bitterness from my heart, looking for ways to affirm him, asking him for input in decisions, and talking with him about issues in my life as he is willing. I will also build a relationship with my pastor and his wife or an older couple as spiritual advisors in my journey.

For a woman committed to restoring purity, there is a significant difference between male relationships pursued in secret and those pursued as a gift from God and with the blessing of spiritual advisors. A woman who has been driven by emptiness and unmet yearnings will need to move from the vulnerable position of forming male relationships on her own to the safer position of forming those relationships with wise input of spiritual advisors.

With solid relationships in place, a woman is in a position

to restore moral purity and rebuild moral character. Though her heart may still have unmet needs, she has a better premise for deciding how to meet those needs wisely. She is better able to recognize temptations for what they are—Satan's tactics to shortchange her. She has a better premise for forming friendships, whether with women or men. And she has the strength and courage to trust the Lord's direction in her life and relationships.

EXERCISES FOR RESTORING RELATIONSHIPS

1. Describe your relationship with your father.

2. If you were able to change one thing in this relationship, what would it be?

3. As you see yourself, what are the ways you have contributed to the problems in your relationship?

4. Here is a list of practical ways for a daughter to build her relationship with her father. Review this list and mark which ones you are doing and which you are not doing. (Note: If you are restoring purity after having been used sexually by your father you will need guidance for restoring boundaries rather than guidance for rebuilding a relationship. You are dealing with invasion rather than vacuum, and the approach must be different.)

   a. Pray for him daily. At the beginning of each week, tell him you will be praying for him and ask him if there are specific things he would like for you to pray about.

   b. Ask him questions about his work and interests. A man's work lies very close to who he is, and your interest in what he does signals interest in who he is.

   c. Compliment him for what he does well. Men respond to admiration. Instinctively they move toward the people/places where they experience being looked up to and they move away from people/places where they are criticized.

d. Ask him for advice/input. This has countless possibilities: your car, your house (or room), anything you own that doesn't work right, your finances, your job, your friendships, your appearance, your hobbies, your ideas/beliefs, your struggles, your plans, your goals, your fears. Don't let "I already know what he'll say" keep you from asking. If your father has been passive and uninvolved in the past, don't be discouraged if you get minimal input—the goal is to treat him like a man more than to get something from him. If your father has seemed controlling in the past and you fear getting drawn into arguments by such openness, determine beforehand only to ask questions. Take his input seriously—write it down, pray about it, and look for ways to follow it.

e. Serve his needs and interests. One way to a man's heart is through pleasing him in tangible ways. Again, the possibilities are many. Prepare his favorite meals and bake his favorite cookies. Clean his car, truck, den, shop, desk, etc. (without discarding or damaging anything, of course). Accommodate his schedule. These are simple ways of saying he is important to you. With all these suggestions, keep clearly in mind that the goal is to begin building the relationship, not so much to change your father. Even what you want from him must be held loosely— if your relationship deepens, wonderful, but if it doesn't, you must be okay with that and still be willing to honor him in the ways you can.

5. Evaluate the above list of ways to honor your father. Which do you find most difficult? Can you tell honestly why it is difficult?

6. Read the section on emptiness in Appendix A. If the activities at the end of that section apply to you, complete those activities.

7. Write out the four resolves regarding relationships.

8. List the ladies in your life who are (or could be) meaningful in mentoring you.

9. List the friends you have that may not be helpful to you in your pursuit of a pure life.

10. Name the pastor and wife or older couple who could help disciple you in your resolve to be restored to purity.

11. Discuss these resolves, one by one, with a godly friend, mentor, or pastor. When you are ready, make each resolve in prayer to God, listing any pointers or thoughts that will be helpful in keeping the resolves.

12. Arrange for periodic meetings with your friend/mentor to discuss your progress.

TO RESTORE PURITY, A WOMAN MUST REBUILD HER SENSE OF WOMANHOOD.

Those who indulge in sexual sin, whether male or female, fall prey to the tactics of the destroyer of our souls. Satan always takes more than he gives—takes it in such measure that our losses mockingly wipe out the thrill of sexual pleasure.

For a woman, a huge loss is her sense of womanhood. God designed the woman to be beautiful. It is a core reality in her being, from the curves of her body to the deeper grace of her bearing and lilt of her spirit. A woman wants to be beautiful—

it is her trump card in relationships. She wants to be attractive. And one of her greatest fears is that she will be plain, ugly, and unattractive.

To be desired by a man is an affirmation of her femininity. To be passionately desired is to be passionately pleased and affirmed. As we noted earlier, for the woman, sex is tied to relationship. If sex is pursued (or permitted) as a means to a relationship, it is viewed as a promise of deep soul-satisfaction to come. And the power of the sexual relationship adds potency to the expectations.

But when passion fades, and when reality sets in that a deep relationship is not part of the package, a woman's disappointment is devastating. She ends up empty-handed and empty-hearted, and besides not having what she really desired, her trump card has been trashed.

She is used. Her beauty has been devoured and wasted. There are no words to describe the sense of loss deep in her womanhood. This is what drove Tamar to wailing and desolation. But Tamar's beauty was robbed against her will. A woman who voluntarily gives her beauty, only to be used and discarded, feels the pain and loss even more deeply.

Her innate sense is that she is now worthless. No real man would ever want her.

This gut feeling, if it is not touched by grace, can pervade her heart and touch all her choices with shame.

Thankfully there is grace.

The grace of God brings hope. Where sin abounds, grace abounds even more (see Romans 5:20). It is true that what might have been cannot be. After sex, neither the man nor the woman will be a virgin again. But when sins are cleansed by the blood of Jesus, purity can be renewed, and a sense of womanhood can be restored. This is the hope Jesus came to give; it is the hope that was realized by Mary Magdalene, by the sinful woman who washed His feet with her tears (Luke 7:37), and by the woman taken in the act of adultery (John 8:1-11).

There is the beauty of being pure—the beauty of a heart that has never been marred. But there is also the beauty of being purified—the beauty of a heart that has been redeemed by grace.

In the beatitudes, Jesus blessed "the pure in heart" (Matthew 5:8). The word He used for "pure" is not the pure of never having been tainted, but *purified,* pure "as being cleansed."[1] How blessed are the purified in heart! *They* shall see God.

This is the blessing a woman who has been involved in sexual sin needs to experience. She can have the beauty of redemption, the beauty of a body and soul reclaimed by grace and rededicated to the service of the Creator.

A woman's beauty is a priceless possession. The beauty of her face, her hair, her eyes, and her form are only the visible features of a beauty that is much deeper and even more powerful. A woman's greatest beauty is in her spirit—and in that "spirit" form, beauty is hard to describe and difficult to measure. It includes the power of her feelings—high and low, broad and deep, from her contagious laughter to her most anguished tears. It includes the quickness and life of her disposition—her responses to people and situations, her grace and depth of feeling, her recognition of what is fine, and her appreciation for everything lovely.

In the presence of a truly beautiful woman, a man can feel clumsy and untutored. A true woman is elegant.

A woman who has given her heart and body to a man illicitly no longer sees herself as truly beautiful. She may know she is attractive, but she feels cheap. If she continues in sexual sin, she will eventually despise her hair, her face, and her figure if the man (or men) who "loves" her loves these surface attractions and not her. When she moves out of that relationship, she is vulnerable not only to seeing herself as cheap, but also to giving herself cheaply in future relationships.

Let's consider grace.

A woman who has been redeemed from sin has been "bought" with the priceless blood of Jesus. In that transaction, she becomes the daughter of God. Whatever her earthly record, whatever her unworthiness, whatever her immaturity, she is a daughter of God by grace. She stands in line to share in His glory, to be ushered with great rejoicing into His eternal presence, to live in the royal, regal splendor of the highest, most noble Personage of time and eternity—the King of all kings and Lord of all lords.

And God accepts her fully, gladly, with great celebration. There is no reluctance in making her His daughter. He does so with sincere delight. She is His because He has become hers. We are recognizing *unworthy* here, but we are also declaring *reality*. This is not a mystical possibility. It is a certain, Biblically-declared reality. She is His daughter!

If you are a lady and have given your body to a man in illicit sexual relationship, if you have done so once or twice or times past counting, your body can be reclaimed by grace. Paul wrote a stirring letter to the Corinthian church—a group of people made up of former fornicators, adulterers, idolaters, homosexuals, thieves, and drunkards (see 1 Corinthians 6:9-11).[2] Acknowledging that sexual sin is against one's "own body," he urged them to "flee fornication." Then he said, "What? know ye not that your body is the temple of the Holy Ghost which is in you, which ye have of God, and ye are not your own? For ye are bought with a price: therefore glorify God in your body, and in your spirit, which are God's" (1 Corinthians 6:19, 20).

If you have been redeemed by Jesus' blood, you belong to God. You have been elevated to royalty. Unworthiness forbids pride in yourself, but it also urges intense gratitude and the utmost care, now, of your body. It belongs to God. Its beauty, its power, its attraction, its uses are now to be aligned with the One who lives in you.

You are not trash. You are no longer defiled. The glory of God is on your life. The purposes of God most High will forevermore direct the uses of your body. You are not to treat your body as though it were used and worthless—it has been bought and it is now owned by the Triune God. Jesus is not ashamed to live in you, and you are not to be ashamed of His house. You are to take care of it with utmost diligence. You are not to speak condescendingly about your body. You are not even to think disrespectfully about Jesus' house. Rather, you are to begin to adorn it according to His directions for you.

Here are His guidelines for His daughters:

1. A woman's body is the visible part of who she is.
2. She is to keep her body and appearance decorous— in good taste.
3. She is not to value herself primarily by her body's attractiveness.
4. She is not to adorn her body to draw attention to it— with jewels, costly clothes, etc.
5. She is to focus on being beautiful in spirit—she is to make herself attractive with such qualities as kindness, faithfulness, quiet reserve, cheerfulness, purity, and integrity.
6. She is to reserve the sexuality of her body exclusively for her husband.

A woman who has been involved in sexual sin will have a heightened awareness of the power of physical attractiveness. She will be more physically self-aware. The danger is to become more preoccupied with her physical appearance. Furthermore, when the realization of sin hits her (as a believer), she may be even further tempted to long for physical beauty—because she feels so physically wasted. God doesn't despise physical beauty. He made women to be beautiful. But He doesn't want His daughters consumed with their appearance, and particularly He doesn't want them to use "add-on" adornments. He wants them to be beautiful at the core of their being.

A woman who has been rescued from moral impurity and restored to moral purity has the beauty of redemption on her life. She is a woman of grace. She is the King's daughter. She is not loud and proud and bold with her face and figure. Nor does she quietly invite or quickly accept the attentions of men. She is grateful, humble, full of faith, devoted, and *purified*. There is an exceptional beauty in such a woman. But she learns discretion and proper reserve. The King within establishes her worth and restores her dignity, and she will not give herself to any man except by the King's direction.

EXERCISES FOR RESTORING WOMANHOOD

1. As clearly as you can, tell how sin has affected your view of yourself.

2. To what extent are those perspectives or evaluations still with you or still controlling you? Another way of exploring this is to ask, How has the grace of God altered your view of yourself?

3. Based on the truth of the Bible (not necessarily your

feelings), write out a detailed description of how God views you.

4. In your own words, describe what would make your "house" beautiful for Jesus to live in.

5. Name and describe any obsessions you have had with your appearance (hair, face, figure, clothes, shoes, exercise). What directions would the King have for you?

6. Name specific qualities you most yearn for as a woman designed to be a "home" for Jesus, and tell why you yearn for those qualities. Discuss with your mentor how those qualities might be developed in your life.

7. What would it take to make you feel truly feminine? (Explore this question to identify any other areas that need work in restoring your sense of femininity.)

8. Write out your commitment to adorn your spirit and reserve your body according to the King's directions.

ENDNOTES

CHAPTER 1: UNDERSTANDING TEMPTATION

1. Scripture taken from the HOLY BIBLE, NEW INTERNATIONAL VERSION®. Copyright © 1973, 1978, 1984 International Bible Society. Used by permission of Zondervan. All rights reserved.

2. Gallagher, Steve, *At the Altar of Sexual Idolatry*. (Pure Life Ministries, Dry Ridge, Kentucky, 2000), p. 190.

CHAPTER 3: IDENTIFYING UNDERLYING ISSUES

1. In a brief released in April, 1998, by the National Center for Educational Statistics, for example, the following statistics were given: "Nearly one third of students get mostly A's when their fathers are highly involved in their schools compared to 17 percent when their fathers have low levels of involvement in their schools. Even more striking, only 11 percent of 6th through 12th graders have ever been suspended or expelled when their fathers have high levels of involvement in their schools compared to 34 percent when their fathers have low levels of involvement in their schools."

2. These quotes come from the book *Pop Goes the Gospel*, by John Blanchard (Evangelical Press, Herfordshire, England, 1983), see especially Chapter 3. In this book, the author shows not only the intentional themes of sex and rebellion in the

music and lyrics of rock music but also the absurdity of using the same media to communicate the rich, deep truths of the Gospel.

3. Scripture quotation taken from the New American Standard Bible®, Copyright © 1960, 1962, 1963, 1968, 1971, 1972, 1973, 1975, 1977, 1995 by The Lockman Foundation. Used by permission.

CHAPTER 4: REPENTING OF MORAL FAILURE

1. See Genesis 42:11 for an example of how glibly we can state that we are true and can be trusted. Consider how this statement sounded to Joseph. In this light, consider also how the sermons of unfaithful ministers or the testimonies of unfaithful fathers sounds to those who know about (or are the victims of) their secret sexual sins.

2. For specific help on overcoming masturbation, see Appendix A.

CHAPTER 5: REBUILDING MORAL CHARACTER

1. Scripture taken from the HOLY BIBLE, NEW INTER-NATIONAL VERSION®. Copyright © 1973, 1978, 1984 International Bible Society. Used by permission of Zondervan. All rights reserved.

2. For more help to understand and deal with homosexu-ality, see Appendix B.

3. This is the bottom line of Randy Alcorn's book *The Purity Principle*. (Multnomah, Sisters, Oregon, 2003). "Purity is always smart; impurity is always stupid," p. 16.

CHAPTER 6: WORKING THROUGH CONSEQUENCES

1. Alcorn, pp. 22, 23.

CHAPTER 7: LIVING A PURE LIFE

1. Scripture quotations taken from the Amplified® Bible, Copyright © 1954, 1958, 1962, 1964, 1965, 1987 by The Lockman Foundation. Used by permission.

2. From Richard Mummau's "Personal Testimony," given at Harmony Christian Fellowship, 1997. Cassette tapes available from Richard E. Mummau, 606 Connie Dr., Mount Joy, PA 17552.

3. See Alcorn, especially Chapter 3, "Getting Radical." In talking about giving up such things as television, cable, or sensual reading, he asks the question, "When we are being entertained by evil, how can we hate it?" p. 63. Later he puts things in even clearer perspective: "Followers of Jesus have endured torture and given their lives in obedience to Him. And we're whining about giving up *cable?*" pp. 68, 69.

4. Alcorn, p. 66.

APPENDIX A: THE PROBLEM OF MASTURBATION

1. Scripture quotations taken from the Amplified® Bible, Copyright © 1954, 1958, 1962, 1964, 1965, 1987 by The Lockman Foundation Used by permission.

APPENDIX B: HOMOSEXUALITY

1. Scripture taken from the HOLY BIBLE, NEW INTERNATIONAL VERSION®. Copyright © 1973, 1978, 1984 International Bible Society. Used by permission of Zondervan. All rights reserved.

2. Dallas, Joe, *Is Homosexuality Inborn? What Current Science Really Says,* (Seattle, WA: Exodus International North America, 1993), p. 2.

3. Carlson, Jodi (compiler), *The Truth Comes Out: The Roots and Causes of Male Homosexuality*, (Colorado Springs, 2001, a publication of Focus on the Family) p. 9.

4. As quoted by Carlson, p. 9.

5. Myers, David, *Psychology* (Worth Publishers, New York, 2001), p. 455.

6. Myers, p. 457.

7. Myers, p. 457.

8. Consiglio, William, *Homosexual No More.* (Victor Books, Wheaton, Illinois, 1991), p. 37.

9. Consiglio, p. 38

10. Nicolosi, Joseph, *Reparative Therapy of Male Homosexuality*, pp. 237-264, as quoted by Carlson, p. 21.

11. Mike's story is reported by Carlson, pp. 27-30

APPENDIX C: RESTORING PURITY IN WOMEN

1. Vine, W. E., *An Expository Dictionary of New Testament Words*, (Old Tappan, NJ: Fleming H. Revell Company, 1966). p. 231.

2. Corinthian morals were so low in Paul's day that if a person wished to slur another's morals, he said, "You live like a Corinthian."

Christian Light Publications, Inc., is a nonprofit, conservative Mennonite publishing company providing Christ-centered, Biblical literature including books, Gospel tracts, Sunday school materials, summer Bible school materials, and a full curriculum for Christian day schools and homeschools. Though produced primarily in English, some books, tracts, and school materials are also available in Spanish.

For more information about the ministry of CLP or its publications, or for spiritual help, please contact us at:

Christian Light Publications, Inc.
P. O. Box 1212
Harrisonburg, VA 22803-1212

Telephone—540-434-0768
Fax—540-433-8896
E-mail—info@clp.org
www.clp.org